Rockets Like Rain
A Year in Vietnam

Dale E. Reich

Hellgate Press
Central Point, Oregon

Rockets Like Rain: A Year in Vietnam

Hellgate Press
An Imprint of PSI Research
P.O. Box 3727
Central Point, Oregon 97502

info@psi-research.com

Book cover by J.C. Young

Library of Congress Cataloging-in-Publication Data

Reich, Dale
   Rockets Like Rain : A Year in Vietnam / Dale E. Reich
      p.cm.
   Includes index.
   ISBN 1-55571-615-6 (paper)
   1. Vietnamese Conflict, 1961-1975—Personal narratives, American. 2. Vietnamese
Conflict, 1961-1975—Veterans—Wisconsin—Oconomowoc. 3. Reich, Dale Everett. I.
Title.

DS559.5 .R45 2001
959.704'3'092—dc21

                                                                        2001024972

Printed and bound in the United States of America

First Edition 10 9 8 7 6 5 4 3 2 1

The Author

Dale Reich was born and raised in the little community of Oconomowoc, Wisconsin. After graduating from high school in 1965, he began to study for a career in law at the University of Wisconsin. Two years later, he volunteered for the draft. He left for Vietnam in June, 1968 to begin his one-year tour of duty as an Army infantryman.

He became a writer in Vietnam, and worked as the co-editor of the official newspaper of the 11th Infantry Brigade of the Americal Division, the same division that produced Colin Powell and Norman Schwartzkopf, as well as the infamous My Lai Massacre. His articles eventually appeared in newspapers all over Southeast Asia. He received both the Combat Infantry Badge and the Army Commendation Medal for his service.

Reich returned from the war to earn a bachelor's degree in Journalism and a combined master's degree in history and education. He has worked as both a weekly newspaper editor and a college public information officer. He has written five books, and his features, editorials, columns and photos have won a long list of awards from organizations like the National Newspaper Association, the Wisconsin Newspaper Association, the Council for Wisconsin Writers, the American Legion Auxiliary, and the University of Wisconsin System. He is currently working on two additional books and a screenplay.

Reich teaches at Gateway Technical College in Elkhorn, Wisconsin, and continues to work as a freelance writer and photographer.

iv

Contents

Foreword – vii

Preface – ix

Chapter 1 - From Campus to Combat – 1

Chapter 2 - Doesn't Anyone Care? – 5

Chapter 3 - Death: Odds At 5-1 – 15

Chapter 4 - Land of Shattered Images – 33

Chapter 5 - To Kill, Or Not – 51

Chapter 6 - The Helter-Skelter War – 85

Chapter 7 - A Dream Comes True – 103

Chapter 8 - Rockets, Like Rain – 121

Chapter 9 - Three Days To Freedom – 133

Chapter 10 - Winners And Losers – 137

Glossary – 141

Let no one forget; let nothing be forgotten.
Perhaps if people do remember, they will act in a spirit of
friendship and brotherly love; and will learn that to
survive they must repudiate war as they have repudiated
cannibalism and slavery.

It is for all who remain to fulfill the ideals and hopes
for which those men lived, not the assumptions for which
they died. Such fulfillment can be their ultimate legacy.

Foreword

The Vietnam War remains a mystery to so many of those who were born when this country's longest war finally ended for the United States in 1973. Despite all the movies and the books and the television documentaries, the truth about this perplexing war remains shrouded in stereotypes, rumors, political rhetoric, and even the desire of some people to justify their actions and beliefs by bending the history of Vietnam to fit their own needs.

Dale Reich provides a fresh and remarkably candid look at the war through the eyes of a young, naive, middle-class draftee whose life was forever changed by what he saw and what he did in Vietnam. His autobiographical book, *Rockets Like Rain*, takes the reader on a powerful adventure and lays bare the pain of having his naivete and his idealism dragged through the mud of wartime reality. Reading his incredibly moving words took me back to my own days in Vietnam as a sergeant in an armored unit. I also served in the Americal Division, and that's why this book provided me with so many vivid and haunting memories of life in the jungle, and of the same firebases where each of us were stationed during our respective tours in the Central Highlands of Vietnam.

This book tells it like it is. It's a valuable insight into those eternal and ongoing wartime clashes between fear and cowardice, good and evil, and right and wrong. It's the story of how the veneer of civilization can be torn away by the need to survive, and by the absence of the rules and norms which ordinarily define a civilized people.

Dale Reich witnessed the same disturbing behavior by young American men that I saw during my tour of duty, including some who were moved to unthinkable acts against the enemy, and to unconscionable acts against their fellow soldiers. Others showed remarkable courage and resilience. All were thrown together in a cauldron of violence that dared them to survive, and challenged them to do things that people who have never witnessed war can only imagine.

Dale Reich's book is more than an autobiography. It's an accurate portrayal of the life of a typical combat soldier told with startling detail, uncommon honesty, and remarkable insight. It penetrates the truth like no Vietnam book before it, and puts the reader directly into his combat boots as he struggles through his 365 days in a war that produced no recognizable heroes and left an entire country both fascinated and perplexed.

This is a book that has taken me on a belated but incredible journey back to my own tour of Vietnam. It's my story as well as Dale Reich's story, and certainly the story of hundreds of thousands of other Vietnam veterans, too.

If you want to have one book on your shelf that explains this complex and still misunderstood war, that book should be *Rockets Like Rain*.

Bruce Kelly

Vietnam Veteran, 1969-70

Bronze Star with Oak Leaf Cluster

Preface

War is often a profound and life-changing experience, and that was certainly true for me. When my students ask me about Vietnam, I tell them it was both the worst year and the best year of my life. I spent much of it in the jungles of Southeast Asia, battling miserable living conditions as well as an enemy that could be both invisible and deadly.

Vietnam served up a long list of extremes for me: hunger and thirst, dirt and disease, loneliness and alienation, and narrow escapes from death both in combat and on a hospital bed fighting a stubborn case of malaria. All of these extremes caused misery and sometimes pushed me to the limit, but they also allowed me to better understand my own strength, patience, and endurance. For that opportunity, I am forever grateful.

Today, with Vietnam as my measuring stick, I am deeply aware of the significance of living in a country that's free and prosperous. I understand the safety and the convenience that others might take for granted. I revel in my wartime survival, and consider each day since I came home on June 6, 1969, to be both a bonus and a blessing.

I am also grateful that my two sons have never been forced to experience war firsthand. The lessons learned there certainly can be invaluable, but the risk is simply too great. No veteran wants his or her child, or the anyone else's child, to perish on some foreign battle-field, even if the war is totally necessary and the sacrifice would be required to keep the rest of us free.

I wrote this book to help my sons and their generation to better understand what Vietnam was really like for a typical draftee, one who left with high ideals and came home smudged with the indelible mark of wartime reality. It's an honest and accurate account that many people will find surprisingly, and many others will find disturbing.

While this book is meant to help every reader better understand what it was like to serve in a complex jungle war, it's my hope that young people will find it especially enlightening. They're the ones who have grown up in a culture that has often distorted or neglected the American experience in Vietnam. This book puts readers into the boots of a combat soldier and invites them to examine the same moral and ethical questions that I faced during my one-year tour of duty.

Finally, I wish to extend my most sincere gratitude to Mr. Emmett Ramey of Hellgate Press for his decision to put this book into print again, and to breathe new life into a story many consider both valuable and timeless. Obviously, he feels the same way. For that I owe him a huge debt of gratitude.

Dale Everett Reich

To my mother and father

Daybreak in Vietnam

The sun filters quietly through the trees.

The ground is moist, fresh and clean.

The grass waves silently in the breeze

and reflects the purity of Nature's green.

A vast sea of blue appears in the sky.

with a crimson border to the east.

A soldier lifts his weary eye

to see the dark of night has ceased.

A pensive, restful mood prevails;

there's no sign of war.

But soon the ears of Vietnam

will hear the cannon's roar.

Dale Everett Reich

January, 1969

Chapter 1
From Campus to Combat

I sat silently in a darkened room in historic Bascom Hall on the University of Wisconsin campus that sunny afternoon, waiting for a group of strangers to decide my fate. Finally, a kindly, middle-aged woman slipped through the door and stood before me. It was written all over her face.

"I'm sorry," she said. "They've rejected your appeal."

It was all over. I had officially flunked out of college.

"What are you going to do now?" she asked quietly.

I looked up through my surprise and humiliation.

"I guess I'm going to get drafted and go to Vietnam and get killed," I said, unable to hide my bitterness.

The woman smiled nervously and walked away.

ʘ

I had lasted for just three semesters. I had known the end was in sight for several weeks, but a kid from the room next to mine in the dormitory had already flunked out twice, and both times the appeals committee forgave him. And his grades had been worse than mine, at least the first time around. His success at remaining in school had given me a false sense of security.

Getting the bad news that afternoon really shocked me. It not only threw me out of school for a full year, but it meant that I could no longer hide behind my 2-S deferment. Military service now seemed inevitable. And with the war in Vietnam going full steam, it was a sobering time. Thank God, I thought, I had three semesters of college under my belt. If I did get drafted it was likely that I would spend my two years punching a typewriter in some dusty, out-of-the-way base in the states. According to rumor, only the uneducated and less-intelligent men went to Vietnam. Those of us with a reasonable IQ and a little education were safe.

My parents were so embarrassed over my removal from school that they didn't even tell my grandparents. After all, they had been used to a fairly steady diet of success stories in high school. My grades put me in the top quarter of my graduating class, which was only a modest accomplishment, but I also had a highly successful speech career, winning several medals and attending two state debate tournaments. I had also gone to Badger Boys State, and I even played on the varsity baseball team for two years.

Now I had let them down, and I was filled with shame and guilt. All I could do was try to find a job to keep myself busy until the draft came knocking. I went back to the factory where I had worked the summer before as a janitor, but the manager wouldn't even take my application. He said I belonged in college. I didn't have the courage to tell him what happened.

My parents finally helped me land a job with a house painter. I started in March 1967. The contractor was a gruff, uncompromising man of about 50. Even his sons refused to work for him. He paid me two bucks an hour, and promised to teach me the trade. He knew I was 1-A, but he was desperate for help. After he harassed me for two months, I finally quit and went to work for another contractor.

The draft board shocked me by letting me run free for so many months. It wasn't until September that I was finally called in for a physical. It was a sign that my freedom was about to end. It may have been the reason why I caught a sudden case of back-to-school fever a week or so later.

I got up one morning with plans to find another college and reapply for my 2-S deferment. Madison still didn't want me until January 1969, but I was sure I could get into a little, two-year teachers college about 30 miles north of Oconomowoc. I figured I could work part-time and commute from home to save money.

For the first time in months I felt as though things were finally going to work out. I remember racing downstairs in my paint coveralls to tell my mother and father about my idea. My mother was still upstairs dressing, but I caught my father in the kitchen. I told him about the two-year college, about commuting, and about the chance to regain my deferment. He listened, but he didn't say a word until I had finished.

"Go ahead," he said crisply, "If you want to be a draft dodger."

I stood there for several seconds, embarrassed by the silence. I was shocked by his attitude. It was so unexpected. I had no idea he felt that way. After all, we had never even talked about what was right or wrong with the draft and the war. I picked up my old gray lunch pail and walked out the door. I never thought again about going back to college before January.

In October I quit my job. For several weeks I bummed in Madison, living with two old friends in their Mifflin Street apartment. I slept on the living room floor, usually until noon, and paid them $10 a week. I also chipped in on meals. Occasionally I picked up an odd painting job that kept me from going broke, but the couple of hundred dollars I had brought from Oconomowoc was rapidly running out. It was obvious that I would have to return home shortly.

I was saved from the humiliation of dragging home with my tail between my legs when my parents called and said they needed me to help them finish their new home. It needed paint, inside and out. It was the best news in months. I drove home that same night and started working the next morning. My parents needed me for the only real skill I had ever learned, and it felt good. But as the house began to take shape that old feeling of uncertainty returned. With my physical behind me each trip to the mailbox was a traumatic experience. I dreaded the sight of any mail that looked like it had come from a government agency. For obvious reasons, Sunday was my only day to relax.

The tension and the guilt that I had once felt, living in the same house with my mother and father, slowly built to its old level. We didn't seem to be able to communicate. I still hadn't made up for the embarrassment I had heaped on them by failing in school. I couldn't even come up with a decent excuse, but they knew what had happened. I didn't attend most of my classes, and I squandered my money at the bars. I had insisted during my last year in high school that I had to go to Madison, even though my parents weren't so sure it was the right choice.

But the more they questioned my decision, the more I insisted. They finally relented, and off I went to give the big university a try.

Not surprisingly, a lot of my friends who also went to Madison were hanging by a thread. Those who had gone to the state school, however, seemed to be thriving. The evidence was overwhelming. I had made a colossal mistake, and I just couldn't take the "I told you so" attitude. They never really said it, but somehow, I knew it was on their mind.

My self-respect fell to an all-time low. I was in the mood for doing something drastic.

In November I mentioned to them that I was thinking about going into the Army. They listened silently. I thought, for the first time, they had finally given up on me.

A week later I drove my 1959 Chevy to the county courthouse and volunteered for the draft. The thought of going into the Army frightened me, but I desperately needed something to put purpose back into my life. The Army seemed to provide me with a golden opportunity. I felt relieved.

Chapter 2
Doesn't Anyone Care?

We flew from Milwaukee to Fr. Campbell, Kentucky, and sat in a classroom filling out forms until after midnight. The next day most of the company had KP, including me. We began around 6:00 A.M., putting out breakfast for dozens of men in uniform while we worked in our civilian clothes. We washed dishes and buffed floors until almost 9:00 P.M., with the smell of kitchen grease following us like a stray dog as we headed back to the barracks.

I drew KP the following day, and the day after that, until I thought I would be doing it for the next two years. I was finally issued a uniform at the end of the first week, and around December 20 we were all allowed to go home for Christmas.

I took a bus to Florida where my family was vacationing. It was a happy reunion. The tensions of the past seemed well behind us. We finally drove back to Ft. Campbell where I spent New Year's Eve lying in my bunk listening to music from the past year. It was a lonely and depressing time, but it passed quickly.

At first I feared the Army and basic training, but I soon learned to thrive on it. I earned the third highest score in the company on the physical training test, outdistancing some 200 other men. I didn't do badly on the rifle range, either, narrowly missing "expert." I liked the feel of clean fatigues and the glisten of freshly polished boots, the crisp saluting and the close order marching. I found that the regimentation gave me a new sense of security. There was no individual thinking involved. Success was guaranteed by conforming to the rules. They were there in black and white—only those who wouldn't, or couldn't take orders, got into trouble.

Around the sixth week, orders for advanced training came down. I was still confident, right up to the last minute, that I was destined to become a crack Army clerk-typist. But I was one of only nine men in the company listed "infantry" when the sheet was hung in the company headquarters. Worse yet, I was one of a handful of men destined for training at Ft. Polk, Louisiana.

Fort Polk was the one place everyone had hoped to avoid. Its infantry unit was called "Tigerland," appropriately named because it was where the Army trained men for jungle combat.

From there it was a short jump to Vietnam.

The surprise of getting orders for Louisiana was bad enough, but now I had to break it to my parents. I had already assured them, by letter and by phone, that I was in no danger of going overseas. I sat down the next day and wrote a letter explaining that there was now a chance—although slim—that I would end up in Vietnam. I thought I was being subtle, but there was no need to mention it again. They both knew what was happening.

Tigerland turned out to be no worse than basic. It concentrated on claymore mines, booby traps, field navigation, jungle diseases, weaponry, and naturally, physical training. Added to that was generous dose of not-so-subtle propaganda. They began to call us "troops," not trainees, and sometimes even the term "queen of battle" popped up. They said we were the ultimate weapon, the trump card that decided every war. Air and ground attacks could soften an enemy position, but it was up to the infantry to take it for good. Infantrymen won medals and rode in ticker tape parades. They represented all that was good and right about the American fighting forces.

I tried to be objective, but it wasn't easy, not after arguing for months that the American position on Vietnam was right. I liked being a part of an Army that was spearheading the fight for democracy in Vietnam. I believed the domino theory with all my heart; I was convinced that the creeping cancer of Soviet communism had to be halted in Asia before it made its way to the shores of California. Ft. Polk seemed like a healthy expression of my patriotism. I wasn't prepared to die, and I was sure I wasn't going to die, but the potential glory that Vietnam held left me nearly intoxicated. I was a minor Superman, a true American, a patriot standing steadfast in the face of enemies at home and abroad. My self-confidence, shattered after Madison, was making a strong comeback. I felt as thought I was riding a glorious current of American destiny. I even dreamed of winning a medal and coming home a hero. I was ready for Vietnam.

ʘʀ

Canada had never really been a reasonable option. I was afraid, all right, but in 1968 there was still too much shame in running away from the service. Canada was a place for criminals and cowards. Decent American men, even if they were bothered by the politics of Vietnam, answered the draft without question. At least most of them did. But it was funny. A man could do everything in his power to avoid the draft back home, but running off to Canada seemed like the ultimate sin. I remember now that the "average" men in my graduating class usually ended up in uniform, while scores of the football players somehow managed to get deferments. That trick knee that worked so well through ten games suddenly became too painful to walk on when it came time for the physical exam. I remember one classmate who sat next to me as I waited in Waukesha, literally shaking in his chair with fear. I felt revulsion at the sight of a 250-pound football lineman cowering like a baby in the face of the draft. He ended up with a 4-F. He had high blood pressure. I think he went on to play semi-pro ball.

That treasured 4-F was like a ticket from Heaven. I had hoped for one on my own because of an asthmatic condition, but I had never been treated by a doctor, so I was declared 1-A. I accepted my fate with a fair amount of courage. I had played the game out, waiting patiently for the draft board to take me, and it had finally happened. I was ready, almost from the beginning, to take what-ever came with my draft papers.

ʘʀ

I remember Steve Wesphal like he was standing in front of me today. He was a well-build farm kid with sandy hair and a big, square jaw. He had muscular shoulders and a smile that was half shy and half brash. He was always joking, always loose.

He graduated from Oconomowoc High School in 1966, one year after me, and the same year my brother Steve graduated. The three of us played baseball together in two or three summer leagues. We shared long hours riding to and from games, cracking jokes and tossing casual insults at one another. He was one of those people no one disliked, someone who seemed to glide through life as though he had a free pass.

I didn't think much about him going into the Marine Corps until my mother called me at Ft. Polk one evening and said he had been killed in action. A rocket, or a mortar, had landed near him, spraying a piece of deadly shrapnel into his head. He died the day after being wounded at Hue during the Tet Offensive.

Steve Wesphal was the first man to die that I knew personally. Even Bob Lutz—whose death came while I was in basic training— was barely more than an acquaintance. We met just as he left for the Marines, and he too, was a member of my brother's graduating class.

Others had died, but Steve's death, more than any other, made the war seem real and very close. My mother, who delivered the bad news during my sixth week of training at Polk, seemed incredibly calm on the phone. I think she was experiencing some sort of low-grade shock, the kind that saves people from insanity when a situation becomes intolerable. I knew that Vietnam was closing in on her too, and I fumbled to reassure her that everything was still running smoothly. I was infantry, and I was going to Vietnam, but the battle was still being carried by the Marines. Wesphal and Lutz, I reminded her, were both Marines. They were the aggressors, the ones who took enemy land and turned it over to the Army for security. The chances of my being killed were small. She could be thankful, I said, that I hadn't joined the Marines.

ᐃ

I had always thought about killing, ever since the whole subject of the war first came up during high school. I had been taught in Sunday school, week after week, that killing was a sin. The one exception, besides self-defense, was killing in war. There, duty was involved. In a sense, that was self-defense too. Defending yourself or your country, it didn't matter. And God only fought on one side. I always pictured him as a kind of honorary American, sort of a powerful Uncle Sam, always there to ensure an American victory.

During my participation in dozens of debates back in the lounge in my Madison dorm, with our emotions piqued by beer and an occasional draft notice, the subject was covered in great detail. Killing, to some, was an absolute: it was always wrong. It had a peaceful ring to it, but it was too pat, too convenient for a kid of 19 who worried about getting drafted.

I always argued that killing and murder were two different things, and that the old rules didn't apply to war. To reject killing was to reject the whole idea of war, and that seemed absurd. War was a part of our heritage. Still, I wondered about how much of what I was saying really had conviction. As a Christian, how did I ever get myself into the position of defending something as heinous as killing?

Not only did I worry about the rightness or wrongness of killing, but I also wondered about how I would react to the sight a of man—or woman—whose life had just been terminated by a bullet from my own gun. One day in training in Louisiana, while a platoon of us sat in bleachers beneath a stand of tall pines listening to a lecture on booby traps, someone asked the Vietnam vet who was delivering the talk what it was like to kill another human being, a Vietnamese in particular.

He winced a he looked, tilted his head and asked: "Ever shoot a deer?

"Yeh."

"That's what it's like. You shoot him and he falls. Just like shooting a deer."

ജ

Only 10 men were selected from our company of 200 to take three more weeks of training on armored personnel carriers at Ft. Knox, Kentucky. The rest received 30-day leaves, with orders after the leave for Vietnam.

Getting that extra three weeks in the states was a terrible disappointment. I wanted to begin my tour, to get it over with. I envied those who would be going 21 days earlier, only because they would be coming home 21 days sooner. Training had done something to me. It had molded my psyche, heightening my aggressiveness until I was actually bursting with a desire to hunt the enemy, to feel my M-16 kicking rapidly as I emptied its rounds. I was caught up in a new insanity. I felt as though I could be trained no more. I was ready for Vietnam now, not in three weeks.

The chance to go home came after nearly 20 weeks of non-stop training. For some reason, those of us who had gone to Ft. Knox got a 15-day leave, half what the other men in our company at Polk had received. We had learned in three weeks how to maneuver APCs and we were ready for a rest.

The last thing we were told as we left Knox was that we were unlikely to use our new skills in Vietnam.

"You'll be lucky if you ever see an APC over there," said one of the training sergeants.

Back home things looked much the same. Everyone was busy. During the day I drove around in a new Mustang I had rented, looking for familiar faces. It was almost futile. Colleges were still in session, and everyone was off in some corner studying for finals. The only one I could find was Reg Weide, my old high school debate partner, who was completing a term at a state college.

Throughout high school Reg and I were best of friends. We had debated together for four years. We also spent a lot of our non-school time together, shooting pool or cruising the street in his father's old Ford wagon. We both went to Madison, and although Reg never flunked out, he came close. He ended up at the state college, commuting part-time and working to keep himself in school. Occasionally he lost his 2-S deferment, but he was overweight, and whenever another physical came close he'd stuff himself to get over the limit, usually with bananas. He played second-string fullback during our freshman year in high school.

School finally ended, and Reg set out each day to line up a construction job for the summer. I tagged along, mostly because I had nothing else to do. After dark we'd jump into the Mustang and head for the bars, or the pool hall, and drink beer until 1:00 A.M. If it hadn't been for Reg, I probably would have thrown in the towel and begun my tour a few days early. Except for Reg, and my family, I was alone, and I knew it.

Sometimes I would run into someone else I knew, in the bars or on the street downtown, and the reaction was usually the same. People were friendly enough, sometimes outgoing, until I told them I was on leave and heading for a one-year tour in Vietnam. Suddenly they would shrink away, looking at me as though I was already dead. Vietnam, like cancer, was suddenly a terminal disease. It left me angry and frustrated. I felt like I was carrying the burden of the war by myself. There was no antagonism back home, but there was no support either. No one wanted to talk about it, or even think about it. But I could think of little else. Now I was experiencing the shock of knowing that my hometown, of all things, was trying to ignore what was going on in Vietnam. Only an occasional intrusion, like a soldier on leave, broke through the facade.

My 15 days in Oconomowoc left me slightly embittered. What I had come to expect from my hometown was no longer there, if it had ever been there. Now I was forced to reevaluate my thinking. Was there some noble purpose to what I was doing, or had I just been suckered into uniform? Did it really matter that men were dying in Vietnam, except to their families? Was there chance, after all, that my death might have absolutely no meaning? I decided to put it out of my mind. Something was wrong, but there was no time to figure out what it was. I had to concentrate on getting myself home alive. Nothing, after all, mattered more than that.

ೞ

The last day of my leave arrived with a great abruptness. I woke up around 8:00 A.M., slightly hung over from the night before, but too filled with anticipation to go back to sleep. My brother, Steve, was standing at the mirror, getting ready for work at the radio station. He worked there part-time, helping to pay his way through college. He grabbed his jacket and headed for the door.

"See you later," he said.

"Yup. See you next year."

Steve stopped at the door, surprised. He hadn't been aware that I was catching a plane that afternoon for California. He turned and stared.

"I guess so," he said quietly.

I just lay there, pretending like I was going away for a long weekend. It was nothing. I was tough enough to take care of myself. He didn't have to worry. I'd be back.

Steve slipped through the door, closing it quietly behind him.

That afternoon my parents took me for a final tour of Oconomowoc in their new, red Buick convertible. We looked at homes around the lake, and talked about everything except what was on our minds. Then, with incredible clumsiness, I blurted out something that had no place in our conversation. Nor did I have any right to say it in their presence. But I said it anyway.

"If I get zapped over there, you get $10,000."

I hated myself immediately. It was the worst possible thing to say. It was horrible. I had jumped ahead of talk about real estate and Oconomowoc and our family, and thrown the worst of it right into their faces.

"We don't want to talk about that," my mother said, trying to scold me a bit. She straightened up quickly. Her lips drew together. My father didn't say a word. He just kept looking straight ahead and driving.

Later we picked up my sister Pam, and my twin brothers, Jeff and Jon, and headed for the airport in Milwaukee. I had nothing to carry but a duffle bag. I was dressed in my khakis.

They finally called for my plane to board, and the six of us stepped through the gate just 15 feet short of the entry ramp. I walked through first, and as I turned, I saw my mother's face begin to melt. She was looking at the floor, but there was no hiding her agony. She was breaking into a million pieces. She seemed more sensitive, more fragile than ever before. Up until that time she had managed to pretend that nothing unusual was happening. But now it was all very clear. She was saying good-bye to her oldest son, and she didn't want to face it.

I felt a rush of guilt. It was my fault that this was happening. If it hadn't been for my pride, I might be sitting in a classroom, nestled snugly behind a 2-S deferment. I was causing my mother this horrible pain. I wanted to wrap my arms around her, and comfort her, and tell her that it was all a big mistake, that I wasn't really in the Army and that I wasn't going to Vietnam. I wanted to tell her that we could turn around and go home.

But I couldn't do any of those things. And now that I was older—grown beyond boyhood—kissing my mother wasn't possible. It was a sign of weakness. Grown men allowed their mothers to kiss them, but they weren't allowed any emotions of their own. She reached up and kissed me gently on the cheek. I stood there like a wooden soldier, still pretending that there was no need to worry, still acting as though it was nothing more than a long vacation.

My father reached out and shook my hand. He smiled gently.

"Good luck," he said. "See you next year"

My sister, then 15, and my little brother, both 13, stood by, smiling with some embarrassment. All three of them were still strangers, people who were living in the same house but leading very different lives from mine. I suddenly realized that I hadn't talked seriously with them, about anything, for years.

I walked onto the plane, too afraid to look back.

ଔ

Less than six months after being drafted I was on a plane heading for Vietnam. Although I was scared, I was excited at the same time. My whole Army experience still seemed like some exotic adventure. I was going to Southeast Asia by way of Alaska, and coming back in twelve months by way of Hawaii. There would also be stops in Okinawa and Tokyo, places I would otherwise never have seen. The Army had promised me travel, and now it was making good on that promise. I was impressed.

There were about 165 of us on that Tiger Airline jet, all dressed in new fatigues and shiny jungle boots. Weapons and helmets and the rest of our gear were to be issued once we landed in Ben Hoa. It was an 18-hour trip, a long time to be thinking about what might lie ahead, and a painfully long time to be thinking about what we were leaving behind.

Just 24 hours earlier, as I flew from Los Angeles to San Francisco, the pilot announced that someone had just gunned down Bobby Kennedy after he won the California primary. I spent my last night in the states keeping his death vigil on a television in my hotel room. It was almost too much to take. Just two months earlier someone had murdered Martin Luther King in Memphis, an event that nearly sent my company from Tigerland to New Orleans to stand by for rioting. I kept thinking about how sick my country seemed to be. Even though I was going to Vietnam, I felt a slight relief at leaving so much trouble behind.

And Vietnam, after all, wasn't going to be a totally negative experience. The war still had the support of our government, and according to the polls, most of the American people. It was a war to save man's greatest treasure, democracy, and to keep 17 million people from the grip of man's greatest nemesis, communism. It was a war, for me at least, with the grandest purpose. I was a glistening knight on a white horse, riding to the glorious front with the Stars and Stripes waving majestically in the background. I was part of one of the most honorable chapters in American history, one of a small percentage of American men privileged to see military duty in time of war. It was a special kind of status, one that more than equaled the self-esteem I had lost by flunking out of school.

What bothered me most, of course, was the thought of perishing overseas. I saw before me, more than once, my broken body lying in a silk-lined coffin, sitting at the front of my parents' church on a hot summer afternoon. But worse than that was the thought of two Army sergeants arriving at my home in an olive drab Ford, coming to tell my family that I had been killed in action. The thought of my family facing my death bothered me much more than death itself. If death concluded suffering for the deceased, I thought, it surely increased it for the living.

I remembered too, on that long plane ride, about my Grandfather Reich and his devastating experience in World War I. He died of unknown causes just a year before I was born. He had joined the Army in 1917 and ended up in a trench in France with the infantry. He survived, but only after suffering through a mustard gas attack that left unsightly burns on his skin and damage to his optic nerve which eventually caused him to go blind.

My father never talked much about him. It was depressing time for his family, not only because my grandfather was slowly going blind, but because the government had refused to recognize that his injury was service-related. For months after getting the news from a South Dakota clinic that his blindness was inevitable, my grandfather and his family worked desperately to convince the government that the mustard gas attack in France was the culprit. There were dozens of affidavits from friends and relatives, but it was no use. My grandfather's records had been lost when his hospital burned to the ground overseas. The irony was obvious. He had given his eyesight for his country, and then denied disability payments by the same country. He died in 1946 at the age of 52, after watching his family struggle along on $40 a month.

My grandfather had always warned my father to avoid serving in the Army and the infantry. When World War II came along, my father joined the Navy. In 1967, 50 years after my grandfather got on a boat to go to France, my father gave me the same advice. I nearly took it. For two months I toyed with the idea of joining the Navy Reserve unit in Milwaukee, but on the night that I was to be inducted I decided to take my chances on the draft. Naturally, I often thought about the wisdom of that decision.

But it was a moot question, now that I was on the way to Vietnam. There was no turning back. All the decisions that needed to be made were already behind me. There was nothing left to do but concentrate on surviving for a year. I laid back and closed my eyes. The pop music blaring into my earpieces numbed me into a kind of uneasy sleep.

Chapter 3
Death: Odds At 5 – 1

Word spread quickly through the plane when someone first spotted Vietnam lying beyond the vast, blue waters of the South China Sea. Several men rushed to the window to get a glimpse. Others, some of them returning for their second or third tours, sat quietly, somewhat amused at the anticipation of the others.

I half-expected to see our plane surrounded by a black burst of smoke, enemy flak greeting us like the American bombers experienced over Germany during World War II. I thought, for a time at least, that we would be whisked off the plane and hustled into some underground bunker to be outfitted with helmets, grenades, and shiny new M-16s. I was ready for 365 days of combat, day and night, if that's what Vietnam had to offer.

But there was none of that. The sun was shining brightly as the plane gave up its altitude to the grubby, rolling hills that lay just beyond the coast. They were peaceful and empty. There was no sight of life until the plane overtook an unending sea of tin-roofed shacks just a mile or two from the airstrip at Ben Hoa. They were incredibly close together, and the plane flew over the shacks so quickly that I barely noticed the Vietnamese walking among them.

As we sat in our air-conditioned plane the stewardess announced over the loudspeaker that the temperature outside was 91 degrees. She wished us luck, and ushered us onto the runway.

Within minutes we were rolling through the muddy streets of Ben Hoa, the smell of cooking rice and swirling dust mixing to create a kind of musty odor that swept through the wire mesh windows on our bus. Just below us were the Vietnamese civilians, people of all ages, bobbing along on their bare feet with their woven, conical hats protecting them from the hot sun and the stares of the new soldiers rumbling by in the big olive drab bus. There was barely enough room for both the bus and the swarming civilians, on the narrow road that cut through the city.

Most of the hootches were a mixture of bamboo, straw, sheets of tin, and plywood which had probably been salvaged from some nearby American dump. The whole scene was straight out of a fourth grade geography book. It seemed so unreal, but there it was, a lifestyle so different from mine that I could do nothing but stare until the bus finally rolled into an American camp a few miles from the airport.

The transfer station, although dirty and rather foul smelling, resembled camps back home. The buildings were made from plywood, some single story structures, and others, like barracks back in the states, rose two stories high. The camp was surrounded by bunkers. On one side was the ramshackle city of Ben Hoa. On the other side was a vast, grassy plain that ended mysteriously at a brush-covered hill. I stared at the hill for several minutes, wondering what it was hiding. I finally came to the conclusion that we were literally perched on the edge of the war.

Army food was always greasy, but the food at Ben Hoa was worse than usual. I stood in line for lunch until I could no longer take the smell. I ended up eating a can of corn curls and drinking a beer, both sold at a tiny booth in the center of the base. It was manned by Vietnamese civilians. Like the mess hall, it was besieged by flies. I pretended not to notice them.

The whole scene was beginning to depress me a bit. Not only was the little compound less than clean, it was downright dingy. I couldn't even find a decent magazine to occupy my time while I waited for my orders. Somehow, around 4:00 P.M., I stumbled into a little building near the mess hall where I heard music playing. It was the enlisted men's club, and a five-piece Vietnamese band was playing "The Lion Sleeps Tonight." I sat and drank a couple of beers, talking with two other GIs who were plotting to "discover" the band and take it home where they could help it earn some "real money." They were dreamers, of course, but Vietnam was a place for dreamers. Most of us believed that once they war ended Vietnam would be trans-formed into a prime resort area, complete with super highways and giant hotels overlooking the ocean. We were, after all, going to win the war. We always won our wars. It was just a question of time.

The three of us walked outside half an hour later, and one of the others pointed to the second story of a nearby barracks. Its corner had been chewed out by an enemy mortar round, killing two men as they slept in their bunks. I stood there staring for several minutes. I knew that men were dying in Vietnam, and for the first time I was learning how. I was glad that my bunk was on the first floor, several feet from the doorway that opened toward the grassy field to the north.

That night I was called for guard duty in a bunker along Highway 1. A specialist 4 who had been in Vietnam for several months joined me and another new man around 7:00 P.M. We split the night into two-hour shifts. He drew the first watch, but I couldn't sleep. We sat in a pair of old metal chairs, propping our feet up with our M-16s resting between our legs.

He was one of the lucky ones. He had spent his entire tour as a clerk typist. Guard duty, he said, was the closest he got to combat. He said, though, that the Tet Offensive was something he never wanted to experience again.

"See that over there?" he said asked, pointing to a gently rolling hill some 300 yards beyond the road. "They were all over out there. I never saw anything like it. We killed about 20 VC right in front of the gate."

"I don't think you have to worry, though. The gooks have to be off the road by dark. If they're not, they know what happens. We blow 'em away."

He was a short-timer with something like 60 days left to go on his tour. That impressed me. After all, I had better than 360 days left. But he didn't seem to think it put him any closer to home than me. After all, he said, another clerk who had just 24 hours to go spent the night hiding under his bunk. A surprise mortar attack dropped a round on the bunk, killing him instantly.

"You never know you've made it until you get on that plane in Cam Ranh Bay," he said.

ʘ

The next day I showered off the dust and headed back to the barracks to wait for my orders. Around noon I was called for guard again and sent to a bunker on the northern perimeter. As I approached, a man inside jumped up and started gathering his poncho and ammo belt. We met at the doorway.

It was David Price, a kid from Oconomowoc who had been drafted on the same day that I was. He had just received his orders for the Ninth Division near Saigon. We shook hands, and I gave him some assurance that his new outfit was one of the best in Vietnam, at least according to its reputation. That seemed to give him a lift, and he shook my hand a second time before walking away. I told him I'd see him back in Oconomowoc in a year.

Dave and I had first met along Highway 67, just south of Oconomowoc, about a year earlier. My old Chevy had stopped running three miles from home, and Dave was the only driver to stop and offer his help. He pushed my car about a mile before we gave up. We left the Chevy and drove to town in his beat up, rusty old Ford.

On December 8, 1967, we were inducted together in Milwaukee. Now by coincidence, we had seen each other for one last time before going to our respective divisions.

Dave was one man who didn't belong in Vietnam. He had gone to work after high school, making himself a prime target for the draft. But while he was struggling through an apprenticeship, I was hiding in Madison behind my deferment, entertaining myself with moralistic debates about the war. I doubt that Dave ever thought about whether or not the whole Vietnam thing was right or wrong. He didn't have much interest in philosophy or politics. All he knew was that a draft order meant that he had to serve, that his life was going to be interrupted by two years of military service.

I could at least attach some meaning to the war, rationalize it, give it a definition. But I don't think David could. He seemed terribly out of place, as much as anyone I have ever known, an innocent bystander, a victim of the times and his own youth. It was hard to imagine he could raise a gun and kill anyone. His innocence, I was sure, made him much more vulnerable than most.

I wanted more than anything to get into a division that had a reputation for toughness in Vietnam. I guess I thought that a hard-nosed division somehow took fewer casualties, or that its reputation might cause the VC or NVA to fear it, maybe even to avoid angering it by making contact.

Of course there was no such division. But it still bothered me to be assigned to the only division in Vietnam I hadn't even heard of. The Americal Division? It didn't matter that it was the biggest in Vietnam, or that its name made it distinctive. It sounded like some kind of Boy Scout troop. I hadn't come across a single Americal veteran in 20 weeks of training. I feared it was so new that it would follow in the footsteps of the Fourth Division, getting itself kicked into sawdust until it learned the ropes. Added to my ignominious assignment was the fact that I was heading for I Corps, hundreds of miles from Saigon, somewhere up where the Marines got shellacked during Tet. I was edgy with fear once again, but more anxious than ever to see just what I had gotten myself into.

Most of the men around me retained their optimistic, characteristically human outlook that someone else was going to die in Vietnam, not them. But I didn't always share their feeling. I was usually calculating odds, figuring that a lot of men, maybe me, had to come up with a short straw before it was all over. With 550,000 men in Vietnam, and 15,000 dying a year, the average GI had a 1 in 35 chance of getting killed. But we weren't average GIs. We were infantry. According to one training sergeant, it took seven men in the rear to support one man in the field. That left some 75,000 of us to absorb 15,000 deaths during our tour. The odds, then, were actually one in every five that I'd end up getting killed. Suddenly I resented every clerk, every cook, every man in the rear whose odds of making it through their 12-month tours exceeded mine by ten times. Every man, I thought, should have at least six months in the field. It didn't take much training to shoot an M-16. Anyone, with two minutes of instruction, could lay out a claymore mine or put up a trip flare. Why hadn't the Army, after so many years in Vietnam, figured out the same scheme? How could it stick with a system that was so grossly unfair? The thought of such inequality left me angry. Before, I had envied the men in the rear. Now I resented them bitterly.

∞

The Americal Division headquarters was located in Chu Lai, a little village along the coast of the South China Sea that had somehow become the home for a major Army division and one of the busiest airstrips in the entire country. We left our C-130 and boarded trucks for some 11th hour training just a few miles away. Behind us, the huge airport roared with the sound of gigantic jet engines, machines which powered the sleek, needle-nosed aircraft that landed and took off every few minutes.

The sight of them filled me with both fear and awe. They made me feel both secure and insecure. It was good to see the muscle that our side commanded, but I was left wondering what kind of ferocious little men were running around in the jungle and hills beyond the base, men who could fight such a powerful arsenal to a standstill. My anxiety was growing as I got closer and closer to the war.

The division had a little camp situated along the beach where it helped its new replacements learn some of the things they had missed during their training days back in the states. The camp was small, maybe ten acres, and it was guarded on the west by a row of small, grassy hills. There was just a handful of buildings— the mess, headquarters, and a bar. In the center of the camp was a row of tents, each filled with a score of green cots. There were also a half-dozen tin-roofed barracks with plywood floors near the beach. They contained more of the green cots, and again there were no pillows or blankets.

I was assigned to a cot in one of the little barracks, at least to start. Later I found myself sleeping in one of the tents, just 30 feet from the ocean. Nearby was a bunker fashioned from a huge culvert, sunk two-thirds into the ground. Only once during my two weeks at the camp did I ever have to hide there. Even then, around 5:00 A.M., I didn't wake up until the rockets had landed hundreds of yards away. I rushed off to the culvert for a couple of quick cigarettes and then wandered back to my cot for a final hour of sleep. I was glad I had missed the action.

During the day we were broken into groups and either given lectures or walked through some stilted training exercises. The lectures were delivered as we sat on bleachers facing the ocean. During one of them the commander of the entire division, a two-star general, stopped by to give us a pep talk about the war. He said it was being won, particularly in the America's zone. He told us the division had a kill ratio of 15 to 1.

That was good, I thought. It compared quite favorable with other divisions. It bolstered my respect for the Americal considerably, and suddenly I felt better about being shipped up north.

Most of the lectures were dull, so dull that the only way we stayed awake was by watching the antics of the giant lizards that scrambled among the palm trees nearby. They were stealthy hunters, stalking insects with tremendous efficiency. They gave the camp a kind of pleasant, exotic atmosphere. It was easy to forget about the war as we sat near the ocean, watching them scramble about in the hot sand. Our morale stayed high during those easy-going weeks. We still hadn't seen anything in Vietnam to shake our innocence.

One of the best things about the camp was the price of beer. It sold for 15 cents a can. It was the same for soda. On most nights I drank several beers and sat on some shaky, weather-worn bleachers watching movies that were shown in the middle of the little camp.

One night a group of us ran into a kid who had been in the country for four months. He was returning from the hospital where he had been treated for a minor shrapnel wound. He was a skinny kid, like me, rather tall and about 19 years old. Because he'd already been in the field, and seen some combat, we crowded around him like a bunch of wide-eyed kids waiting for some major leaguer to sign his name to our autograph book. We bought him beer and bombarded him with questions. We wanted to know, more than anything, what it was really like in the field. He ate up the attention, gladly trading war stories for beer.

Our hero said he had taken a piece of shrapnel on his right elbow. He displayed a small scar, explaining how much the metal burned before he brushed it off with his hand. He said he was heading back to his unit in the field in a day or two.

Before he left he told one story that stuck with me. He said he was riding with a group of GIs on the top of an APC one afternoon when it stumbled onto a boy about 15, running parallel and about 50 feet from the track. At the time our man was carrying a grenade launcher, an M-79, and at the urging of his fellow soldiers he loaded a round and aimed it at the young Vietnamese. The round caught his victim in the neck, tearing his head off.

Our young hero laughed. He obviously wanted to impress us with his tough, nonchalant attitude. A few of us smiled back. For several seconds no one said anything. I finished my beer and went back to my cot.

During the day the camp got incredibly hot. The sand caught and held the sun's radiation until it seemed as though we were going to boil in our own sweat. The tents and the barracks offered little relief. For the few men who spent their afternoons swimming in the ocean, even a 30-second walk on the beach could quickly turn into second-degree burns. Only nightfall, with a cool breeze from the ocean and cold beer from the bar, brought any relief.

During my final night in the camp I got into my first fight in years. Everyone was standing in line at the beer counter, waiting for their turn to buy a beer for themselves and their buddies. As usual, the line was long, and the wait was 15 minutes or more.

While I stood in line that evening, just two or three men from the counter, a big African-American GI in a white T-shirt walked to the front and ordered six Budweisers. No one said a word. The men around me had apparently noticed his huge arms and the impatience on his face. He was probably a cook or a clerk, assigned to the camp permanently and most likely given permission to get his beer when his day ended.

But I didn't think about any of those things as I stood there. He had offended my sense of fair play, and I asked him why he didn't get in line like everyone else. He told me to mind my own business. I repeated my question, and he backed into a fighter's stance. He raised his fists and told me he'd bust my jaw if I said another word.

Now my ego was involved. I had gotten myself into a terrible corner. I was too embarrassed not to call his bluff. I started to repeat my question for the third time, but a quick roundhouse from his massive left arm suddenly had me ducking. Unfortunately, I ducked too late. His fist caught the top half of my right ear. It was a glancing blow, and I popped back up to see him standing there, almost in tears, his face taut with anger.

I was stunned, not by the blow, but by his reaction. He looked like any angry child. His hurt was so deep that it showed at a glance. For a second I pitied him. I felt like the straw that broke the camel's back. I stared at him as he challenged me to jump the fence and finish it.

There was no question in my mind that I wasn't going to take up his challenge. I had no intention of forcing the issue any further. It didn't mean that much to me.

In a second I felt blood dripping down the side of my neck and onto my shoulder. Without hesitating I turned and walked around the long line and headed toward my barracks. When I couldn't stop the bleeding I went to the medics tent and ended up with a conspicuous bandage wrapped around my ear.

That night I watched the movie, hoping I wouldn't see the same man again while I was in camp. I drank several beers and ate about a dozen Slim Jims. In the morning, just before several of us boarded a deuce-and-a-half to be shipped out to our battalions, I got sick. The truck waited while I fell to my knees, throwing up undigested grease. In a minute I joined the group as we headed to the airport for a ride to a place called Duc Pho.

◌੪

As the C-130 rumbled down the runway on its way to Duc Pho. I thought about what a short, overweight lifer had said one night in Chu Lai about the 11th Brigade, which was stationed at Duc Pho. He said one of its battalions had been "wiped out" the week before, and that we were destined to take their place in the field. He laughed when he said it, but we all knew there was probably some truth to his teasing.

I slept for about an hour on the plane. I woke up just as Duc Pho came into sight. At first glimpse it looked like just another firebase in the middle of the Vietnamese countryside. To the west were huge hills, almost mountains, blue-green and covered with thick vegetation. To the east, about a mile beyond some trees and thick foliage, was the ocean. As we stepped onto the mesh runway we were confronted with a large hill in the middle of the base camp. It seemed to rise from nowhere, steep and sprinkled with large rocks. At the top was a big antenna and a few bunkers.

We were broken into small groups and sent in several different directions. About six of us were escorted to an isolated bunker at the base of the big hill. There a second lieutenant welcomed us to the 4th battalion, 3rd infantry, and told us we would then be broken down into companies. I ended up in D Company. In a few minutes I was standing in front of a row of tents, each surrounded by its own five-foot high wall of sandbags to guard against rocket and mortar attacks. Over the door of each tent was a wooden sign, hand painted, which identified the company and its headquarters.

I walked inside and found a baby-faced company clerk behind a gray metal desk. I told him that I had been assigned to D Company. He called to the first sergeant, who answered from behind a plywood wall at the rear of the tent. A big blond man with a neatly-trimmed flattop finally pushed aside a curtain fashioned from an old Army blanket and stepped into the room. We shook hands, and he ordered the clerk and another man to get my gear and get me ready for the field. He said a chopper was leaving with supplies the next morning, and that I would be on it.

I stepped outside and waited for the two men to emerge from the musty old supply tent next door. It was a typically hot, summer

day. The road in front of the row of company tents, beyond the
perimeter maybe 100 yards away, was Highway 1, nothing more
than a two-lane dirt road. Occasionally a jeep or a truck would
rumble by, creating a thick, brown puff of dust that would rise 20
feet above the ground and linger for several seconds before
evaporating. Beyond the road were rice paddies, filled with a
dark green, immature crop. Further west was a row of trees and
foliage. I assumed that was where the enemy was hiding, or at
least where he set up his mortars when he chose to harass the
base camp after dark. I was glad to be safely behind the brigade
perimeter, and thankful for the daylight.

In a few minutes one of the men appeared with a square,
metal frame that had a big knapsack attached to it. I noticed
immediately that the thin metal frame was peppered with little
holes.

"Where did those holes come from?" I asked.

He said it was shrapnel. He couldn't remember which, but the
last man who had the rucksack was either killed or seriously
wounded when he stepped on a booby trap.

I asked where my locker was, and both men laughed.

"That's your locker," one of them said, pointing to the rucksack. "That's your home for the next 12 months. If you want
anything in the field, you'd better put it in there before you go."

After getting my M-16, a poncho, two flares, an ammunition
belt, and a few cans of C-rations, I sat down in front of the
company tent to wait for supper. For the first time since I was
drafted I felt alone, really alone. I was less that 24 hours from the
field and my company, and I knew I wouldn't see one familiar face
when I got there. The company couldn't even provide me with a
locker, or a secure place to put my meager belongings. It was
simply loading me down with supplies and turning me loose.
And worst of all, I was being hitched to the harness of a dead
man. I hadn't known, until then, that I was really superstitious.
But I didn't want that rucksack. It was bad luck. The whole
encounter with D Company was leaving me scared and depressed.

I sat in the hot sun for several minutes, too crushed by what I
had found in Duc Pho to move into the shade. Suddenly the clerk
popped through the door and handed me a clean, white business
envelope. I recognized the letter by the "Reich Realty Company"
logo in the upper left hand corner.

The last thing I expected, for several days at least, was mail. But there it was, a lifesaver tossed to a man drowning in self-pity. I opened it carefully and read it several times.

It didn't contain much news. It was one of those letters a father writes his son to let him know that he hasn't been forgotten back home. It was neatly typed, like all of my father's letters, and written with an empathy that can only be shared by men who have gone off to serve in the military. It was short on news, but long on reassurance. I carried it for days, reading it whenever I got a break.

I had never felt closer to my father, probably because he understood, more than anyone back home, just what I was going through. He never knew until I got home how much that letter meant to me, but our relationship was never the same again. That letter, and the war, and the year away from home, were giving us a new and deeper relationship. It seemed incredible that a single, typewritten sheet of paper could do so much that day. I was glad the change had come, but terribly afraid that it had come too late. I still had eleven months to go, a long time to steer away from the booby traps and the bullets that were waiting up ahead.

After supper—cold cuts and beans served in the mess hall by Vietnamese civilians—I found out that my chopper would be delayed for 24 hours. I didn't mind, of course. It was all good time. It was another day I wouldn't have to spend in the field.

The next day, after spending a night on a dirty green cot in the supply tent, one of the men in the company who was also waiting for a ride out to the field invited me to take a tour of the village. It sounded like a good way to pass time.

Duc Pho ran north and south, straddling Highway 1. Its homes and shops were fashioned from bamboo poles and woven mats that served as walls and curtains. A few hootches had plywood floors, and some even had electricity. The village smelled of dust and diesel fuel and baking bread. I decided I wouldn't eat anything while I was there, but I did need a haircut. We stopped at a barbershop in the middle of a village and I sat down on an old, wooden chair.

There was no door or wall in the front of the little hootch. Trucks and jeeps whizzed by just a few feet away. The barber was an old man with thin white whiskers streaming from his chin. He was nervous, but friendly, always smiling and shaking his head in agreement. He apparently didn't understand any English. A young girl, perhaps 15, was standing in the doorway that led to the rear of the hootch. She was thin and pretty, dressed in shiny black pajama bottoms and a white shirt. A tiny gold earring adorned each side of her head. A small boy sat next to me chattering away in a mixture of English and Vietnamese. In the background an old record player was churning out American pop music.

My friend left for a minute, which made me uneasy, but he soon reappeared, holding two cold cans of Budweiser. I drank mine quickly, and we sent the boy for two more, and two more after that. When the barber finished I gave him a dollar. He bowed and gave it to the girl, who disappeared into the back room. We sat and drank for a few more minutes, until the boy finally coaxed us into walking down the road about 50 yards to see a "real VC."

The beer suddenly hit me as I stepped outside into the sunlight. I was high, almost to the point of forgetting exactly where I was. The boy pulled me by the hand until we were standing over the body of a young man about 18 years of age. He was dressed in nothing but a loincloth, and his body was growing puffy in the hot afternoon sun. His skin, smooth and brown, was stretched tightly. He looked like a mannequin that had been tipped over, almost plastic in appearance and perfectly still. There were no marks on his body, no bullet holes or shrapnel wounds that were visible. He was lying on his back, and his eyes were closed. Flies bounced around his mouth, ignoring the children who kicked at the corpse and poked it with sticks to amuse one another.

I stood there for several minutes, fascinated by the aura of death. The corpse reminded me of the funerals I had attended back home, the first for my great-grandmother when I was barely seven years old. A year later a friend, then just nine, toppled from a tractor and was killed. That second funeral haunted me for months. I imagined him lying under my bed at night, waiting to grab my hand if I let it drop to the side. I always slept with my arms tucked beneath me, afraid that if my friend grabbed my arm I would be drawn into the supernatural, too.

The sight of that ripened body overcame the beer and snapped me back to reality. The fact that a corpse was rotting in the middle of the village didn't bother me. I understood that it served as a warning to other Vietcong. What fascinated me was death itself.

I told my friend I had seen enough of Du Pho, and in a few minutes we were back inside the compound. I slept soundly that night, even though a ride to the field was less than twelve hours away.

After leaving Duc Pho on a supply chopper I ended up on a dusty little firebase somewhere along Highway 1 near Chu Lai. I spent the night in a bunker with two men from a different battalion. We didn't even introduce ourselves. We were, after all, just strangers passing in opposite directions. All that was necessary was an agreement to divide the night's watch into three equal parts, which we did.

The two men talked for about an hour. Most of their conversation revolved around a company that got credit for 300 enemy kills, even though most of the dead were women and children. They laughed at the gullibility of the men in the rear, and mentioned two names, Pinkville and My Lai. It all meant nothing to me. I smoked a couple of cigarettes and fell asleep.

The following day I caught a chopper to the field to join my company. I ended up on a tall hill well off Highway 1. It overlooked several square miles of rice paddies, broken only by an occasional oasis of palm trees.

I got there in mid-afternoon, along with another man who was reporting to the same company for the first time. We were eventually assigned to the same platoon. His name was Carlson, and he stood barely 5 foot 6 inches, the same height as my brother, Steve. He had sandy hair and freckles. His head was half hidden under a helmet that looked to be two sizes too big.

I could see the anxiety on his face, and imagined that I looked much the same. It was like joining a little league team for the first time. I felt horribly awkward, while everyone around us seemed so at ease. We drew a couple of prolonged looks, but in a few seconds everyone went back to their business.

Vietnam was full of strangers. Back home we usually ignored strangers, and the war didn't change any of that. GIs went about their business as though Vietnam was a normal experience. They didn't rush up to greet one another simply because they wore the same uniform. The time and effort needed to invest in a friendship was carefully allocated, just as it was in the states.

Carlson and I left the chopper pad and headed for an underground bunker in the middle of the firebase. We descended a short flight of stairs where we were greeted by a young

lieutenant. He introduced us to our sergeant, who smiled at the
sight of two new bodies to help replenish his platoon.

"Sir, I have just the place for them," he said, "I need a good
M-79 man and somebody to carry our mine detector."

I stood there, embarrassed to be a full head taller than
Carlson. It didn't take me long to figure out which of us was
going to get the mine detector.

Carlson was overjoyed with his M-79. I think it was because
he didn't have to carry the detector. That evening they brought
me the detector, complete with batteries. It was broken down so
that it could be carried easily by a man humping along in the
jungle with a weapon, and a rucksack riding on his back. By the
time I stuffed most of it into the rucksack there wasn't much
room for food or flares. The batteries, enclosed in a case about the
size of a shoebox, rested neatly in my left pants pocket. They
were connected to the detection plate by an insulated wire. The
earphones were flexible enough to be crammed into the rucksack
without damage.

The whole encounter made me as mad as hell, though I kept it
to myself. I had the most inglorious assignment in the company.
The detector seemed so out of place with the rest of my
surroundings. Maybe it was the fact that it appeared to put me in
the greatest danger that upset me. I knew I would have to walk
ahead of the other men, listening for the right sound that might
give away a carefully buried mine. While I risked my neck, the
rest of the company could be 100 feet behind me, waiting for
something to happen, safe from the ravages of the bullet-like
shrapnel. I felt like a guinea pig, a newcomer being stuck with the
dirtiest job.

But I had no choice. There was no appeal. I decided to try to
make peace with my new companion, and to take each assignment as it came.

That night, after supper, I found my platoon, seated in a circle
in a far corner of the firebase. Most of the men were sitting
Indian-style, with their legs crossed and their feet tucked tightly,
passing around a cigarette. As I sat down a couple of them stared
menacingly. No one said a word. I wondered if I was in the right
platoon. For several seconds the circle was quiet. Then someone
looked at me and asked, "Are you C.I.D.?"

"No," I said, somewhat surprised.

"Are you sure you aren't C.I.D.?" said another man.

I denied it again. For one thing, I didn't know what they were talking about.

"He isn't C.I.D.," said a third man, putting the issue to rest.

The cigarette burned out. Someone lit another one and it began its rounds, each man cupping it carefully to hide the burning end. That made sense, I thought. That's the way we were taught to keep the VC from finding our position at night. But why share the same cigarettes?

It took me a while to catch on. The cigarette was marijuana, and it wasn't the VC that worried the platoon, it was the officers. The men didn't want to get busted. Their paranoia was evident. They even talked about finding a C.I.D., a plant sent out among the troops to bust pot smokers, and killing him. It could be done, they reasoned, without much trouble. Men died easily in a firefight. Even a bullet in the back of the head wasn't going to raise a lot of eyebrows. Men panicked under fire, scattering rounds haphazardly. It happened to experienced men as well as newcomers. Besides, who was going to know where the fatal bullet came from?

I smoked one of my own cigarettes and blew up my rubber mattress. I laid down on the hill, marveling at the absolute darkness of the surrounding country-side and the sprinkle of stars overhead. I was learning alot about Vietnam with each passing minute. I was happy that I didn't smoke marijuana, and even happier that I was not a C.I.D.

The morning, like the previous night, was perfectly still. The sun rose quickly, warming the top of the unprotected hill with an intensity that soon made us forget the dampness that had been with us just an hour earlier. The firebase, stripped of its trees and tall grass, was a giant oven. The air hung heavy; there was no wind to wash away the stale smell of the grease and smoke coming from the mess tent.

I almost gave up on breakfast before I got to the tent. I didn't want anything to do with greasy food. But I knew I had to eat, so I managed to down some powdered eggs and a glass of Kool-Aid. After that I headed back to the company area to check my equipment.

We soon found out that our platoon had been assigned to run a patrol to the north that morning, maybe 500 yards out. It was my first patrol, and I was lucky. The sergeant said the mine detector could stay behind. It wouldn't have much use in the field that day. It was a big relief.

We walked about five minutes in silence, winding our way single file through waist-high elephant grass. Beyond the trail in either direction were vast fields of rice paddies.

There didn't seem to be much danger that we would be ambushed, so I concentrated on landmines and trip wires. I carefully followed in the exact footsteps of the man walking ahead of me, making sure that I didn't increase the impressions he had made in the dusty soil.

Suddenly the men in front of me, and a few behind me, started yelling and pointing to the west. In a second some of them were leveling their M-16s and firing. I couldn't see anything through the tall grass. The line had stopped just as I descended into a gully. I raised my weapon in anticipation, but there was nothing to do. No target. Nothing.

In a few seconds it was over. The men in the platoon put their M-16s back on their shoulders and turned north once again. I asked the man behind me what had happened, and he said five young Vietnamese males had been spotted running a couple of hundred yards away.

Did they have weapons? Rucksacks? Anything that made them look like Vietcong?

"They were running, so they were VC," he said.

Vietnam, I learned that day, was like the Old West. We were to shoot first, and ask questions later. Any Vietnamese male old enough to carry a gun was a potential enemy. And potential enemies were practically the same as enemies. They had to be stopped or shot. Maybe both. There was not time to debate anything like murder versus self-defense, or detention versus extermination. There was no grand strategy, no thought of winning converts or protecting innocent civilians. Each man seemed to be taking the narrowest view. His own survival came first, even if his impetuousness might cost a few innocent lives. Whether or not the killing of a single Vietnamese would change the course of the war was debatable. But the need to survive was not. For a man walking around in the field in Vietnam, angry and scared, there was nothing to cling to but his own instincts for survival. For the infantryman, Vietnam had reduced life to its most basic terms.

We walked another ten minutes until we came upon a shelter, a grass roof supported by bamboo poles. Beneath it were a half-dozen women. They didn't' move as we approached. Lying on a mat was a baby, naked and obviously newborn. It was blue—thin, sickly, and obviously near death. In the corner was a girl, around twelve, lying on a dirty, woven mat. Her large brown eyes darted from GI to GI. We stood there gaping. Finally, someone asked, in a combination of broken English and sign language, who the baby belonged to. One of the women pointed to an old mamasan in the corner. She was obviously close to 70. Most of the men laughed. The charade was easy to see through. The young girl had just given birth, and the baby, silent and extremely frail, had just minutes to live.

The other men wandered off to a nearby hootch to look for fresh water. But I stood there, trying to think of something to do or say. Back home I had been taught never to turn my back on suffering. But what was there to do? I couldn't call an ambulance. The choppers would fly in for a wounded or sick GI, but would they bother to pick up a dying Vietnamese child? I finally did what the rest of the men had done. I turned and walked away, hoping that I was wrong about the baby. In a few minutes I forgot all about that desolate little scene.

We made our way back to the firebase without incident, and that night the platoon drew an ambush patrol. Around dusk we headed away from the perimeter and down the hill, making our way along a series of huge, jagged rocks. Suddenly the file of men stopped, and we were ordered to sit down even before we had cleared the hill.

In a minute the word was passed along in whispers that we would spend the night where we were. There would be no ambush, no walking out into the rice paddies to set up a perimeter. Even the men on bunker guard above us on the hill were in on the conspiracy. They fired a few shots over our heads to make it look good just as the daylight faded away. We slept silently that night, and we were never discovered. The next day we marched into camp at daybreak as though we had just come in from a site several hundred meters away.

What we had done was clearly dishonest, but my conscience didn't bother me. Instead of being embarrassed by what had happened, I was happy. I had helped to fool headquarters, and for some reason, it felt good. I had joined a new Army, not just the one fighting the VC, but the one fighting the officers, and NCOs, those who orchestrated the war. The fake ambush turned out to be a brief, hidden victory. But it left me elated. My sanctimonious defense of the war and all its trappings—honor, dignity, truth—conflicted with what I had just done, and it made me a hypocrite. But I felt as though I was being more responsible to myself and my safety. I could never have forgiven myself if I had lost an arm or leg over some foolish, nighttime ambush.

The next day the company headed back to Chu Lai for "stand down," 48 hours of drinking beer and resting.

ల

Aside from the airfield, there wasn't much to see in Chu Lai. There was Highway 1 to the west, and a road leading east toward the ocean. We could see a bunker line a few hundred yards away, and a row of hootches half a mile to the north. That, we were told, was where the prostitutes could be found. But in the day and a half we spent in the battalion area, we didn't go near the hootches. We just drank beer and waited for our next assignment.

Like everywhere else I had been in Vietnam, Chu Lai became black and silent after the sun went down. It magnified my loneliness and isolation. I would have given anything for the reassurance of a neon sign—any kind of lighted sign—something to indicate that Vietnam wasn't as uncivilized as it appeared during that night.

The one bright spot was the music of a skinny GI named Phillips. Somehow he had come up with a guitar, and he was lying on his side in that big tent in the darkness, strumming and singing "Lonesome Town." His music was no better than average, but it seemed awfully comforting. I was suddenly relaxed. Despite the melancholy lyrics, Phillips' song had taken the sting out of that long and unsettling night. I laid back on my rucksack and smoked a cigarette, more at ease than I had felt in months.

But the peace didn't last very long. From the other side of the tent, out of the darkness, came the harsh voice of another GI.

"Shut up over there. We're trying to talk."

Phillips stopped, lying his guitar down quietly. He was too timid to challenge his antagonist.

Chapter 4
Land of
Shattered Images

On July 2 we woke up to a bright Chu Lai sunrise. It was around 7:00 A.M., the usual time for infantrymen to arise. The word had gone around the night before that a mission in the field—no place specific—was about to begin. We were ordered to pack up three days of C-rations for a trip north. No one seemed to know where were going, or what we were going to do once we got there, and no one seemed to care. They just started stuffing C-rations and ammunition and flares into their rucksacks.

As a newcomer I just followed suit. I went to the pile of C-rations boxes a little late, and I paid the price. There wasn't much left but lima beans and ham, beef and potatoes, and a few containers of peanut butter. There wasn't a single can of fruit left in the pile. That reminded me of something a Vietnam vet had told me while I was on leave. He said men would fight over a can of fruit. What I found that morning made me wonder if it was true. I stuffed the leftover cans into my rucksack and walked back to the tent to clean my M-16

The C-ration encounter disturbed me a bit. There was no one around to police the platoon, to make sure that every man got his share of ammunition and food. And worse yet, there was no interest among the men—at least none that I could see—to play fair with one another. It was a simple case of first-come first-serve. It was only human nature, and I knew it. But I didn't like it. The one redeeming thing about going to Vietnam was the camaraderie that I was sure I would find in my infantry platoon. I thought of it as reassuring glue, a fiber woven so deeply into men that it took a war to bring it out. It was beyond human frailty. Only men in combat could experience the feeling, the spiritual uplifting of souls interwoven like the links in a giant, steel chain. War was the great equalizer, and it was that equality which most certainly would bring out the best in every man. At least that's the way I pictured it.

The scene earlier that morning—men scratching through cardboard boxes, trying to beat one another to a few ounces of food—was discomforting, but it wasn't shattering. I still believed that when we faced the enemy, things would be different. Together we'd exhibit strength and courage, risking our lives for one another.

I still thought that we were something special, and when the time came, I was sure we'd prove it.

We sat outside our tent for an hour or so, passing around M-16 cleaning kits. A few of the men read magazines, the girly types that seemed to be lying around wherever we went.

Carlson, perched on his overstuffed rucksack, played with his .45 pistol, stroking it with a soft brush. I watched him for several seconds dusting his toy and admiring his handiwork, before I went back to my own chores. Suddenly, there was a shot, and I looked up just in time to see sand jumping in front of Carlson's feet. His .45 had gone off accidentally, and he was as embarrassed as he was surprised.

"Take that thing away from him," someone said.

He quietly put it back into his holster and lit a cigarette.

Finally the word came around to "saddle up," and we dragged our rucksacks up over our shoulders and settled them as best we could on our back. My rucksack cut into the base of my backbone, and the shoulder straps pulled sharply downward. It wasn't long before I was wedging my thumbs between the straps and my shoulders to relieve the pressure, as I struggled through the deep sand to the dirt road 100 yards away.

The morning heat was beginning to burn through our jungle fatigues. We sat along the road for a few minutes before a deuce-

and-a-half pulled alongside and stopped. In a minute we were heading north along Highway 1, the dust rising behind us like a thick snake. We clung to our M-16s as we rode, watching the civilians passing by on their bikes and on foot.

I wondered how many of them were NVA, filtering south with a fake ID card bearing a photo taken at some military post in North Vietnam. Some, undoubtedly, were NVA soldiers heading toward the population centers. But it didn't matter. We were going in the opposite direction. All I wanted to do—now that I was actually in the war—was make it home. I felt my desire for heroism fading more quickly as each day passed. I no longer wanted to make any bid for a medal. I just wanted to make it home.

The countryside north of Chu Lai seemed particularly beautiful that morning. A soft breeze barely disturbed the lush greenery. Vietnam was hot, but somehow pleasant, and deceptively peaceful. It was hard to believe that the war was still in progress, or even that it had ever come at all. Aside from the trucks and the helmeted men riding down Highway 1, there was no indication of the conflict. Even the civilians, smiling constantly, gave no sign of the struggle.

The truck finally brought us to a large village where other men and machines were waiting. There was a track with a long gun mounted on it, a bulldozer, and a half-dozen APCs. We jumped off the truck, one by one, into a sea of children swarming around the vehicle. They just spoke enough English to ask for candy and cigarettes. A few held out icy cans of Coke. The price, as always, was 50 cents.

We formed a line and headed west between several hootches. The children, showing no fear, each latched onto a GI. The boy next to me was around ten or eleven. He seemed different than the others, quieter and more mature. He had nothing to sell, and he asked for nothing. When he turned I could see that his left eye was missing. In its place was a massive scar. I pointed to my left eye, unable to control my curiosity.

"VC?" I asked.

"No," he answered. "American planes." He made a pass with his hand to indicate that a fighter plane had been responsible for his disability.

He kept staring, and I shrunk with embarrassment. As we approached a river the children fell away from the line of GIs, one by one. When my turn came to cross, I stopped and handed my young friend a can of ham and lima beans. It was my meager way of saying "here's some compensation for your eye, compliments of the American Army."

He took it without saying a word. He just kept staring. I hadn't ever remembered seeing a sadder face. I turned and rushed into the knee-deep water, relieved to have such an uncomfortable encounter behind me.

We must have walked for two or three miles before one of the tracks broke down. It was a problem that would repeat itself again and again. When it happened we just found a spot of shade under some palm trees and sat down to smoke. There was nothing to do but wait.

We were heading dead west. For a while there was a road, somewhat overgrown, but a road nevertheless. Eventually it faded away, and the bulldozer was brought up to the front of the caravan to cut a path. The legendary jungle, the green, man-eating tangle of Asian vines that I had expected to see didn't materialize. Instead there were rice paddies on both sides of the road, and hootches scattered in a most unorganized way. The hootches were there—usually nestled among cool clumps of banana and coconut trees—but there were no people.

At first it seemed eerie, but I came to regard it as a relief. Since virtually all civilians were suspects—either actual or potential Vietcong—their absence allowed me to relax. There was no one to watch or interrogate. There was nothing to do but take advantage of the bulldozer's bad luck.

Toward nightfall we pulled to the side of the road and set up camp. We settled on a tall, grassy hill, and beyond us lay an endless expanse of rice paddies broken only by an occasional hill. They were really little mountains, popping out of the earth abruptly, green and steep. One stood no more than 500 yards beyond our position. Just below us was a cluster of three of four hootches located between several trees. In the center of that tiny village was a well.

We all dug foxholes that night. In training we had been taught that the enemy liked to launch mortar attacks after dark. The only defense was a foxhole, as deep as we could dig it. I was stationed along the perimeter with two other men. We dug a hole about three feet deep and three feet across before we rested. it was obvious that if a mortar attack came, two of us would have to find somewhere else to hide. But the day had been long and hot, and we were bone tired. We decided it wasn't worth our effort to make it any larger.

We drew lots, as usual, to see who would stand guard first. I was lucky. I got the best hours, from dark until about 11:00 P.M. By midnight I would be asleep, with seven or eight hours of rest ahead of me.

But something happened that night that changed my plans. It was nearly black and dead quiet, as usual, and I was too frightened to smoke a cigarette, fearing that the VC might smell the smoke or see the flame and crawl up to slit my throat. I just sat there, my M-16 resting across my lap, scanning as much of the valley as I could see under the stars.

The calm was broken when the man in the next foxhole, about 25 yards away, jumped to his feet and leveled his rifle.

"Halt," he yelled, his voice echoing loudly as it bounced off the nearby hills. Suddenly his M-16 cracked off several rounds, just a second or two after he had yelled. I ran over to ask what he had seen.

"I don't know—when I shot, it rolled down the hill."

"Shouldn't we go down there?"

He looked at me like I was crazy.

"Hell no. Get back over there where you were."

I wasn't about to argue. I knew someone could be lying at the bottom of that hill, bleeding his life away. There was nothing but silence. Maybe he had missed, or maybe he had imagined it. One thing seemed certain. The victim wasn't likely to be a GI, even though several men had descended into the village hours earlier to retrieve water from the well. What was likely was that the poor wretch who wandered up that hill was a civilian, unaware of our presence. His carelessness may have cost him his life.

Later that night the hill in front of us lit up with a multitude of colors. It was another American firebase. I hadn't realized it until that moment that it was the Fourth of July.

The next morning a few of us went down into the village to fill our canteens and check the area for weapons. We searched the hootches and found one male, about 35 years of age, wearing dark pajamas and carrying an ID card that said he was 50. He didn't speak English—at least not that we knew of.

We ordered him out of the hootch to try to determine if he was a VC. He smiled constantly, always willing to do as we said.

I held the ID card for several seconds, staring alternately at the picture and then his face. Suddenly I realized that I didn't know a thing about interrogation. I wanted to believe that he was a South Vietnamese farmer, an innocent civilian unlucky enough to be caught in the path of an American convoy. But his hands were much too soft, and his posture was too erect. It was likely, one of the men said, that he was an NVA officer heading south to join his battalion. But how could we prove it? I was caught between my desire to purge the enemy from among the civilian ranks, and my desire to show the South Vietnamese that we wanted to treat them with respect.

My humanity, or lack of aggressiveness, won out. I handed back the ID card and walked to the well to fill my canteens, frustrated and slightly angry. The convoy soon regrouped and started west once again.

The next day brought more rice paddies and more delays. We were lucky, though. It was the middle of the dry season. A wet road might have bogged us down for days. Finally, around 4:00 P.M., we reached our apparent destination, a small hill covered with thick clumps of vegetation. We cut a path through the center with machetes, and sat down to wait for the bulldozer to begin clearing our new firebase, which was to be called " Karen."

We were ordered to set up a perimeter and dig in for the night. It took a few hours before the bulldozer had completed its work, scraping the top of the hill bare. It unveiled a beautiful panorama below us, a huge valley with a river running north and south through its center. As the sun set it spread an abundance of soft orange colors across the horizon, creating a most impressive sight. Even the best sunsets back home had never come close to what I witnessed that night. It made it easy to forget about the heat, the weight of my rucksack, and even the enemy. It was a surprise, a disarming comfort that seemed completely out of place on such a hot, miserable day in a war zone.

But I was grateful, and I think the other men were too, although none of them mentioned it. We were, for the most part, still strangers. I considered myself a rookie, untested in combat, an unknown quantity to the other men in the platoon. I was anxious to prove myself, to earn their respect. I hoped my chance would come quickly.

That night, after our foxholes were dug and our claymores set out, a group of the men in my platoon sat in a circle at the edge of the perimeter, obviously waiting for a chance to smoke some grass. I wasn't invited along. A day or two earlier they had learned that I was a "juice freak," that I preferred beer to marijuana. That automatically labeled me as an enemy of the pot clique. Unfortunately, the clique was 75 percent of the platoon. I was, in effect, a permanent outcast that the pot smokers were forced to endure, only because I was assigned to the same unit. Happily, there were others, like Carlson, who fit into the same category. I sat with him and another newcomer named McMillan, smoking cigarette and drinking warm beers. No one said much, but we didn't have much in common, either. I kept thinking what a long year it would be if I had to spend it as a minority, clinging to other non-smokers to protect myself from the tyranny of the clique.

That little encounter with the dopers was bad enough, but my whole philosophy about camaraderie among American GIs was shaken that day by still another incident. Several of the men with our infantry company had put their rucksacks on the APCs in the convoy, taking only their M-16s and some ammunition as they walked a protective flank. That night they found that several items had been stolen by the men in the APC units. Radios, stationery, even cans of fruit, had been pilfered. The most upsetting thing, of course was the fact that the thefts had taken place while the men in the infantry were risking their lives to guard the APCs.

The whole episode made me kind of sick. I was beginning to realize, rather quickly, that my year at war wouldn't just involve a confrontation with the enemy. Other Americans were a potential threat as well. I was almost to the point of believing that in a firefight there would be no one to trust but myself. It was a cold thought. I wanted so badly to be part of a cohesive group, dedicated to the survival of all its members. Now I had too many thoughts to re-examine, too many things to re-evaluate. I was never so sorry that I had volunteered for the draft.

Early the next morning the bulldozer smoothed over our end of the perimeter. I talked with the driver for a few minutes after I pulled in my claymores.

"What are those?" I said, pointing to a pile of round, metal objects lying next to the bulldozer.

"Land mines."

"Listen, I walked out there last night with those claymores.

You mean those things were out there then?"

"Yup."

"They're all dead, aren't they?"

He shook his head. "Not all of them."

"You mean I could have gotten my ass blown off?"

He nodded, and we both laughed.

Life on LZ Karen quickly settled into a kind of comfortable routine. I got off my rubber mattress each morning and folded it into a neat package. Then I would down a C-ration breakfast, relieve myself, and head for an underground bunker where the platoon pulled guard along the perimeter. Inside was a level spot where I would lie on my back and go back to sleep. There was little threat of an attack during the day, so no one objected. At least they didn't say anything. Besides, there was simply nothing else to do. I had neither the energy nor the interest to clean my weapon and ammunition, even though both were dusty from the frequent helicopter landings that took place just a few feet away.

Occasionally the monotony was broken by a hot meal that was sent to us on the re-supply choppers. We ate off paper plates and drank cold fruit drinks from paper cups. The hot meals were quite good, and provided a substantial change from C-rations. It was a great boost for our morale. Every few days there was also beer and soda. I sometimes traded my soda for a couple of beers (the going rate in the field was one soda for two beers), and then saved them until 7:00 A.M. That was the coolest part of the day. Temperatures never dropped below 70, but it seemed chilly. Still, the beer was warm in my mouth and almost without taste. I soon gave up that practice.

Karen, of course, had its share of discomforts. The choppers always created little dust storms whenever they landed. The Chinooks were particularly bad. Their blades could literally blow a man over if he came within a dozen feet of the landing pad. The whirlwind could choke him with dust, filling his eyes and nostrils until he slumped to the ground with his head buried in his lap. Naturally the gear in camp suffered as well. Ponchos, jackets, even helmets and weapons were frequently tossed about. Leaving a bandolier of ammunition near the landing zone almost guaranteed a night spent in cleaning hundreds of rounds of M-16 ammunition, one by one.

There were times, too, when there didn't seem to be enough water to go around. A "water buffalo" was usually located near the center of the little camp, maybe 100 yards from any portion of the perimeter. When that ran dry we'd have to watch the skies for a re-supply chopper. Sometimes they didn't come until close to dusk, and that made the sun seem hotter and the time drag mercilessly. If we really found ourselves short we'd often ask the artillery boys for a drink, but they weren't always willing to oblige us. Sometimes they'd let us bake in the sun for hours, guzzling water in front of the grunts as we waited for out chopper. They always seemed to have everything: water, beer, soda, cigarettes, and even ice. They even had rather sophisticated little hootches, built from hundreds of empty shell boxes, and plenty of clean fatigues. It was as though Karen was inhabited by two armies, one well-equipped and one modestly equipped.

We had just one change of clothes in the month I spent on Karen. I stumbled onto a box of fatigues that had come from the company area back in Duc Pho earlier in the day. As usual, I got there late, and picked over the used but clean clothing until I found something that fit. It was funny, I thought, how a man could get used to living with his own dirt and dried sweat for weeks on end without even noticing.

The one place we had to bathe was the river than ran about 600 yards west of us. It was about a hundred yards across and rather swift. It was clear and clean, and it served as a great temptation on days when the water supply ran short and the number of "dust baths" from incoming and outgoing choppers was running high.

Even so, I took just one bath in the river during my month-long stay on Karen.

∝

I didn't really know what we were doing on Karen, and I guess I never really cared. Apparently we were some kind of blocking force, stuck out in the countryside to monitor the movement of NVA from north to south. Karen, with its strategic position, seemed well-suited for the job. We could see for miles to the west, and we had artillery at our disposal with a range of 17 miles or more.

But Karen never took on much significance until I stumbled into the artillery area one night while hunting for an unguarded water buffalo. There, in the center of a small area surrounded by dirt berms, was a pile of brown bones standing maybe three feet high. I stood and stared for several minutes, amazed that the pile contained several human skulls. The bones had been uncovered by the bulldozer when it carved out a spot for the artillery pieces. They were apparently left over from the last war when Vietnam defeated the French in the early 50's.

It was an eerie sight. I was almost certain that the hill had been the site of some massacre. Suddenly Karen seemed small and vulnerable, and I was swept by a feeling of uncertainty. Standing there, next to the pile of bones, left me shaken. I had visions of defending Karen against hordes of attacking, fanatical NVA troops.

As I filled my canteen I scanned the perimeter, standing almost in the middle of the firebase. If an attack came, was there an escape route? Probably not. That's the ironic thing about being in the middle of a perimeter. It was the strongest position possible, but it left no room for escape. In an all-out attack it could be victory or defeat, but there was simply no chance to withdraw. If the NVA wanted to isolate us, they could. Help could come only from the sky, and choppers didn't like to fly into a zone under fire. Karen, which only minutes earlier had been a comfortable haven, now seemed like a kind of prison.

Although it was the dry season in the highlands, there were still occasional periods of heavy rain. Each man was always left to fend for himself when the weather got bad. There were no tents, unless of course a man could create one out of his poncho. I tried that by pounding a metal stake into the ground at an angle and draping my poncho over it. The first time it rained I sat in my newly-devised shelter, cross-legged and fairly dry. But eventually the wind whipped the poncho until it wrapped itself around the stake, leaving me unprotected.

The longer I sat there, the madder I got. I looked a few feet to my right and saw a GI named Tanner staring at me from the protection of a culvert he had gotten from the artillery boys. His little home was six feet long and three feet high, and protected on one end by artillery boxes. It was absolutely moisture-proof.

He sat and watched me for several minutes as I struggled with my poncho. His face showed absolutely no emotion, but his stare made me angry and embarrassed.

I was sure he would eventually invite me to share his shelter, but he just kept staring. What bothered me most was that we were from the same state. We had already met, and he had even shown me a picture of his wife back home. But he just sat there, peering at me like I was a scene from the late, late show.

Finally, my patience and my pride ran dry. I walked over and asked bluntly if I could share his little nest. His lip curled like some child who just had his candy swiped away.

"There isn't enough room," he whined.

I slammed my helmet to the ground, staring angrily for several seconds. The whole scene was ridiculous, and I knew it. I felt like a fool, but I couldn't help myself. I was sure others were watching Tanner and I play out our little scene. I wanted to hide some- place, but where? I sat down, just a few feet from Tanner, and waited for the rain to stop. Mercifully, it ended a few minutes later.

Tanner and I didn't speak to each other for several days.

After a week or so of lounging on the perimeter, we were told that a minor operation was about to take place across the river. They said only that it would last one day, and that packing C- rations would be unnecessary. That pleased everyone. C-rations, in almost any quantity, were heavy, and since humping in the field often destroyed our appetite, we often ended up throwing them away anyhow. That made it especially frustrating. Carrying ham and lima beans for five miles was misery enough, but gagging at the sight of them when we ate was the ultimate misery. Water or a Coke, warm or cold, were all we thought about after carrying a rucksack and dragging our own heavy legs for any distance in Vietnam. The sun had a way of shrinking our stomachs. It made finding something to drink our lone obsession.

We started out humping toward the river at mid-morning. It took about ten minutes before we gathered on the river's edge. There we found that choppers had brought in a score of rubber rafts. It must have been a terrifying sight for the GIs who couldn't swim. Falling overboard with a rucksack and 30 pounds of grenades, flares, and ammunition was almost certain death.

We boarded the rafts, eight men each, and pulled ourselves across the river with a rope that had been strung from one side to the other. It was a slow and clumsy journey. I knew that if the rope broke we would float helplessly down the river. We'd be sitting ducks if a squad of NVA were waiting around the bend. Fortunately, the entire company made it to the other side without incident.

There a few members of our platoon, including me, were chosen to climb a nearby hill and act as a blocking force while the rest of the company swept through the rice paddies and grassy fields to the south. It was perfect duty. All we had to do was sit and wait for the operation to end.

൚

A light rain fell as we watched the operation slowly unfold in the valley hundreds of feet below us. The rice paddies stretched for half a mile, separating our hill and a larger one to the south. I sat down and waited, smoking a cigarette that I cupped in my hands to keep it dry.

I was glad that I didn't have to walk with D Company that day. I was sure the valley was well booby trapped, sprinkled with trip wires and explosives, most of them probably salvaged from dud American artillery rounds. Rewiring a dud was fairly simple, and the VC and NCA were experts. The last thing I wanted was to get hit by shrapnel out in the boonies, miles from the nearest friendly hospital. I hated the thought of dying, but the thought of going home with one or more of my limbs blown off wasn't attractive either. Most of the men who talked about the booby traps said they preferred to die rather than go home with an arm or leg missing. I disagreed, but I understood their feeling. The booby traps obviously did a great deal of psychological, as well as physical damage, which is precisely why they were there in the first place.

Booby traps, I was told, were most often found on the ground. Sometimes they were attached to a trip wire, sometimes to a pressure device. Occasionally the VC detonated the explosives by way of a simple electronic device, almost always stolen from the Americans.

But sometimes the explosives were located in trees, and the VC even put them underwater where GI patrols were likely to pass. Those devices were called "bouncing betties," and they were perhaps the most feared of all. As soon as they emerged a foot or two out of the water they exploded, sending hot shrapnel into their victims.

But for now there was no reason to worry. Someone else was taking the risk. For once I had drawn the long straw.

D Company disappeared around the hill for about 45 minutes, then formed a long line that ran perpendicular to our position. They were walking slowly, obviously thinking about a possible ambush.

Just when most of them came into sight we spotted a

Vietnamese male emerging from an underground bunker in the middle of the rice paddies. He seemed totally unaware of our presence. The men on the hill with me jumped to their feet and began pointing and debating over possible action. Finally, they all decided to open fire.

I didn't shoot. I was sure we were too far away to be effective. All the noise accomplished was to warn him to seek cover. In a second or two he disappeared back into the bunker as rounds struck the dry soil around him.

Almost at that instant bullets began sizzling over our heads. We couldn't hear where the shots were coming from, but we knew we were under fire from the distinctive crack of the rounds as they came through the air. Everyone dropped to the ground. Suddenly we realized that the line of D Company infantrymen across the rice paddies was shooting our way. They had heard our shots and assumed that we were a squad of NVA. Most of them had forgotten where the blocking force had been stationed.

We had virtually no cover. There was simply no place to hide. Someone finally got the idea to pop colored smoke grenades, the kind used to signal choppers at a landing zone. Yellow, purple, green, and red smoke began oozing from the hillside, and the firing stopped.

It was such an absurd situation. One of us could have been killed or wounded, not by enemy fire, but by men from our own company. When it was all over some of the men around me laughed.

D Company circled back to its rafts in a few minutes with a pair of VC suspects. They were both males, 18 to 20 years of age, dressed in black pajama bottoms with white tops. They were frightened, but they offered no resistance. Both of them had their hands tied behind their backs.

A few of us caught a ride up the hill to Karen on the back of an open APC. Among those riding were the prisoners and the men who taken them into custody. As we began our five-minute journey up to Karen a GI started poking one of the suspects in the ribs with the butt of his M-16. The GI just laughed when his victim doubled over in pain, then repeated his taunt. It bothered me to watch, but for some reason I did nothing. Finally, another GI, who was also tired of watching his sadistic buddy, objected to what was going on. His warning was ignored.

The track stopped at the edge of the firebase, and I hopped

off. As I began walking away I turned to see the two GIs standing face to face, with a sergeant mediating their dispute. I felt good about the GI who intervened. I was glad that someone else felt the same way I did. But I also felt ashamed that I didn't have the courage to intervene myself. I had seen a wrong and did nothing to change it.

The next day on Karen I was assigned to help a crew that was stringing concertina wire around the perimeter. We already had about four concentric circles of the barbed wire guarding the firebase, but the captain in charge of the base wanted more. We had to select one man from our platoon for the detail, and the platoon leader chose our squad to provide that man. I was the one who was chosen, and it made me furious. The assignment came from PFC Edwards, my team leader, a 19-year-old kid from Washington state. He chose me because I was the newest member of the squad. That really irritated me, because Tanner had only been in the company two weeks longer. I felt picked on, and I let Edwards know it. But he stuck by his assignment, and I was soon wearing heavy gloves and stretching concertina wire along the side of the hill.

After two hours the detail was over. I returned to the company area and found nothing where my gear had been except for the metal stake I had driven into the ground a few days earlier. Apparently a Chinook had landed, lifting my poncho and rucksack and tossing them in different directions. They were nowhere in sight. My helmet had actually blown beyond the wire and out of the perimeter. It sat halfway down the hill, 50 feet away. My rifle laid on its side, caked with dust. The ammunition, in the same condition, was laying nearby.

I could no longer contain myself. I looked for Edwards and found him with Tanner, lounging about 30 feet away. It was bad enough that the Chinook had torn up my gear, but no one had even bothered to pick it up when the chopper left.

Edwards could see how angry I was, and he stood up in antici- pation. I began to yell a few inches from his face, but he just stood there and stared. Our confrontation lasted no more than a minute, and my anger cooled considerably when I noticed a .45 caliber pistol in his right hand. I walked back to my area, defeated and fairly convinced that the rest of my tour in Vietnam was going to be a disaster. Now Edwards had a reason for sticking me with every dirty, and even dangerous, duty. My tirade had gotten me absolutely nowhere. All I did was let off some steam.

I eventually figured out that it wasn't Edwards who really bothered me. It was the fact that my life was now in the hands of someone else, a boy of 19, someone I didn't like or respect, an amateur playing a game that required professional instincts and judgment. In Vietnam, there apparently wasn't enough experience to go around. It was one place where the responsibility, and the risk, was happily bestowed on the first person willing to take it. Men were given three stripes and a platoon to command, even before they were old enough to shave.

For the first time I felt slightly betrayed about being in Vietnam. I had gladly, perhaps naively, volunteered to enter service and take my chances in a combat zone. The least I expected in return was to have some experienced, responsible leadership. What I got instead was a smart-aleck, pot-smoking kid who reinforced his image by bragging about the women he had conquered. The whole situation was as absurd as it was pitiful. I had no idea what would lie ahead, but I feared that it wouldn't be good.

One story that Edward told always stayed with me. He and a buddy named Smitty had discovered an old man hiding in a bunker in the field one day. They flushed him out, and then ordered him to go back into the bunker, tossing in a grenade behind him. To their surprise, the old man emerged unharmed. They ordered him back again and tossed in another grenade. The old man came out for a second time. Blood was trickling from his ears, but he was still alive. They ordered him into the bunker for a third time, and as he descended they filled his back with bullets.

Edwards always laughed when he finished his story.

◌◌

As I watched the sunset on Karen one evening I almost convinced myself how unlikely it was that any Vietcong or NVA were in the area. Aside from the two suspects, and the man in the bunker across the river, we had seen no signs of human life. The river rolled along peacefully. The rice paddies, now lying fallow, and the thick jungle greenery that surrounded much of the firebase, seemed so quiet. If it hadn't been for the presence of the war, my troubles with Edwards, and the dust, I probably would have felt like a privileged tourist, enjoying the beauty of the highlands.

It lulled me into a false sense of security that was abruptly broken as I slept one night. After dousing myself with mosquito repellent from head to toe, I laid back on my air mattress near the perimeter and drifted off. The nights were cool and comfortable, and sleep came easily.

But that one single night changed everything. I remember waking up suddenly to a thumping noise on the side of the hill, maybe 50 feet away. I looked up and saw dirt being scattered in all directions. It was a mortar attack.

In a matter of seconds I had gathered up my M-16 and ammunition and was firing from the safety of a nearby bunker with several other men. We could see the flashes from the mortar barrel just across the river. We were soon joined by the artillery boys with their big .50 caliber tracer rounds zeroing in on the enemy. In a few seconds the mortars stopped falling, and we breathed a sigh of relief. Then someone reminded us that the mortars might be softening us for a ground attack. We fell silent, each man straining to see through the darkness. It wasn't long before a friendly flare went up from one of our mortar crews, and we concluded that the rounds were simply harassment, a reminder that the war was still in progress.

We stood in the bunker for a few minutes more. Finally we returned to our regular guard schedule, with most of the men slumping back to sleep on their air mattresses.

Fortunately, no one was hurt. The VC had miscalculated. Their rounds all fell short. Next time, we thought, they would be on target. That made a spot in the bunker even more valuable, and most of us were reluctant to leave it at night after that, even for a few minutes.

A few mortar rounds dropped on the side of the hill the following night, but again they did no harm. The men along the perimeter were better prepared this time, and the response came much sooner. Our M-60 machine-gun fire was soon joined by the .50 caliber. It wasn't long before the mortars were silent.

The third night was uneventful, but on the fourth night another attack came around midnight. The VC hadn't learned from their earlier mistakes. The rounds exploded harmlessly in the dirt at the base of the hill.

The harassment, physically harmless but emotionally draining, finally got the young lieutenant in charge of the artillery. Flexing his muscles as the acting commander of LZ Karen, he ordered the 1.75mm cannon to be moved to the west end of the perimeter. He was screaming his orders so loudly that I was sure the VC mortarmen heard every word.

"Get that thing down here," he shouted, "I'm sick of this. . ."

The big gun, its impressive barrel protruding well beyond the front of its carrier, finally maneuvered its way down to the edge of the perimeter.

"Give me some direct fire," the lieutenant screamed, "Down there. Fire at will."

The barrel was lowered slowly. It was pointing directly across the river toward a clump of trees along the bank. Finally it boomed a round, and its noise was deafening. Even with my ears covered by my hands I felt a sharp pain in my head. Still, it was a stimulating event. The biggest thrill was seeing a huge chunk of earth fly into the air where the round struck. In the light of an overhead flare we saw trees toppled under the impact of the gigantic round. Such a display of power made me exuberant. No Fourth of July fireworks ever came close to what that cannon showed me that night.

The first round came fairly close to the area where the lieutenant was pointing, and he immediately ordered his men to load up again. There was simply no way to aim such a weapon accurately, at least not point blank. It was made to work with a computer that zeroed in on targets several miles away. At least that's what the artillery boys had told us. But that night it did what all of us wanted; it frightened the VC into calling off their little attacks. Never again was our stay on Karen interrupted by enemy mortar rounds.

Our next venture from the security of the firebase took us just below the hill to a small group of hootches that were hidden beneath a cluster of trees and vines. It was strange to find the little dwellings at the base of the hill, because I had been on Karen for two weeks and had never even known they were there. It was proof enough that if the VC or NVA wanted to mass an attack from there, particularly after dark, it could be done fairly easily. Although the hootches were deserted, there were a few pigs and chickens scattered throughout the little village. Some of the men shot at them as they scurried by. It was an acceptable way to relieve their frustrations. It wasn't long before we returned to the comfort of our little firebase.

That night we found out that A Company had crossed the river and lost two men in the process. A GI who couldn't swim had plunged into the river with his rucksack on his back before he found out how deep the water was. Soon he was floundering, calling for help. A second man volunteered to tie a rope around his middle and attempt to rescue his buddy.

Both men died when no one on shore held the rope.

Amateurs playing a deadly game. I thought. Death was coming regularly, but not in the ways I had expected. Accidents seemed to be killing more of us than all the mortar attacks, booby traps, and enemy ambushes combined. It was absurd, but it was happening.

The war was making less and less sense to me with each passing day. My earlier concepts were being shattered in a remark-able short time. My clearest thoughts about Vietnam were becoming blurry and gray. The only thought that stayed in focus was my need to get back home alive.

Chapter 5
To Kill, Or Not . . .

Toward the end of July, I woke up one morning to the sound of explosions and gunfire in the distance. Beyond the river and the rice paddies I could see an American jet fighter making passes at a sandy hill. In the middle of the hill was a depression where a Vietcong was apparently hiding. The jet would make a pass, firing its cannon and dropping bombs, and as it headed skyward there would be the sharp and distinctive retort of a rifle. The strange little battle went on for so long that I finally wandered up the hill for water. When I returned the jet was gone. There was no way of telling whether or not it had been successful in killing the VC.

It was such a symbolic battle. Here a VC with an AK-47, or perhaps only an M-1, had created a stalemate with a million dollar jet. The plane was burning fuel, ammunition, and time, and risking its own destruction at the hands of a single enemy soldier who posed little or no immediate threat to Karen. A single, well-placed shot could have brought the jet to earth. It had happened before. Even if the plane killed the VC it was unlikely that anyone was going to hike out to his bunker to confirm the kill. Probable kills, after all, didn't count in the record book. Someone had to stand over the corpse to confirm it.

Apparently the pilot didn't want to fly back to his base with a full payload. Any target, even a lone VC in a reinforced bunker, was better than no target at all.

With nearly three weeks under my belt at Karen, I began to think I might spend most of my tour there. The food was becoming more tolerable, especially since someone had recently come up with a C-ration cookbook. I don't remember who owned it, but I caught on to a recipe for fudge that really gave my meals a lift. It was simple formula: a package of cocoa mixed with peanut butter. I hunted through all of the discarded C-ration boxes and came up with a small pile of the necessary ingredients. After making fudge for three or four straight meals, however, I stopped just before I got sick. I soon returned to eating the rations without mixing them.

Occasionally we'd stumble across some discarded LRRP rations. They usually came from the artillery unit. They were cereal-like and came in little plastic bags. All we had to do was add water. They looked a lot like the ground feed my grandfather fed his cattle back on the farm, but they tasted good after several days on a C-ration diet.

The word was sent down one day that a major mission was about to take the company from its perch on Karen. We didn't know where we were going, as usual, but we were told to saddle up with several day's rations and ammunition. The whole thing had very ominous overtones. There was even a rumor that some platoon in the field had run into a nest of NVA and gotten itself chewed up.

We obediently packed our gear, and soon were filing down the hill and heading north along the river. The afternoon sun was viciously hot. It poured its heat into my uniform, and soon I was soaking wet. My helmet felt like it weighed a hundred pounds. My rucksack, the curse of all infantrymen in Vietnam, cut into my shoulders until I was sure they had been rubbed raw. My M-60 rounds, strung neatly together and riding across my chest Poncho Villa style, jabbed my ribs with every step. Soon I imagined myself to be a stupid burro, absent-mindedly putting one foot in front of the other until someone stopped me.

When the platoon sergeant finally called a break each man struggled to get his rucksack to the ground. A few of the men just collapsed, allowing the rucksacks to cushion their fall. Others freed one arm, and then the other, lowering their burden with great care. One or two of the men just stood there, apparently wondering if it was worth the effort for a five-minute break. Everyone reached immediately for thier warm canteens. A few hardy souls lit up cigarettes.

I remember walking for miles that day. It seemed like we were never going to stop. Along the way, while cutting through heavy jungle toward a clearing along the river, we discovered a group of Vietnamese civilians. They had just finished gathering a small pile of pineapples, which lay at their feet.

As our squad moved up to where they were standing, each man helped himself to the fruit. Then they turned and walked away. I stood there for a moment, watching the civilians. They smiled, probably hoping that we would do nothing more than rob them of their harvest. I took a pineapple as well, but I reached into my rucksack and replaced it with several cans of C-rations.

The Vietnamese made nervous bows and quietly accepted the olive drab cans. I could sense the cool reaction of the GIs around me because of my gesture, but I felt no shame. I suppose the civilians could have been Vietcong informers, or even members of an enemy unit. Maybe they had a secret booby trap factory somewhere nearby. But if that was true, we had to assume that all civilians in the area were working or fighting for the other side. And if that assumption was made, then it was logical to believe that they should all be killed in the interest of the company's safety and the overall war effort.

That was the dilemma. How could we distinguish the good from the bad?

Most American soldiers assumed the worst. Civilians were guilty until proven innocent. But I just couldn't buy that notion. I still believed that most of the people in Vietnam hadn't made their minds up yet. They didn't belong to one side or the other. And stealing their food was hardly a way to convince them to join us. I thought, as I stood there handing out my C-rations, that I might be very naive, even to the point of making a fool of myself, or even aiding the enemy by feeding its supporters.

But if we were to assume that all Vietnamese were Vietcong, then the war was already lost. There was no need to continue fighting, pouring American lives down the drain. It was time to pack our gear and go home.

We set up camp along the river. Our squad was assigned a position about 25 yards ahead of the rest of the company to form a lookout post. We were separated from the river, which was about 40 yards to our left, by a cornfield. It was a strange sight, since there were no hootches or other signs of life nearby. In the

distance, maybe 300 yards away, was Karen, looking terribly
bleak and small. I had never realized how tiny the firebase was
until that moment. Despite that, it gave me some comfort to
know that we were at least within sight of another GI encamp-
ment. There was also the pleasant reminder that Karen's artillery
could come to our aid if things got hot.

We set out our claymores and flares as soon as we dropped
our rucksacks. There was no time for foxholes. Darkness was
upon us, and the company was still organizing for the night. We
hurried through a can or two of rations, then sat down to decide in
what order we'd stand guard.

Suddenly the radio next to me began to buzz with activity. An
ambush of four men was calling back to the commanding officer,
asking for directions. They had spotted a line of enemy infantrymen coming up the trail, the same trail we were scheduled to
take north on the following day. They reported that the NVA had
full packs and AK-47 rifles, and they would soon be upon the
ambush site.

"Listen," I heard the voice of the CO say, "I want you to fire
two clips and get your ass out of there. Got it?"

About 30 seconds later the firing started. It wasn't long before
we realized we were in the line of fire. Bullets began whizzing
around us, and we struggled to bury our heads in the soft ground
along the riverbank. The sudden bursts were followed by small
explosions, obviously grenades. We stayed near the ground and
struggled to see in the darkness. The trail and ambush site were
no more than 75 yards north of us.

The four men from the ambush had dropped some of the NVA
in their barrage, and luckily they avoided any injuries themselves.
To everyone's surprise they reported that the grenades had come
from the NVA, not the Americans. The enemy, we thought, had
stayed cool in a tight situation. We figured we were up against
experienced, hard-core NVA. It was a chilling, but inescapable,
conclusion.

That night was a nervous time for everyone. Our position was
probably compromised by the ambush, and without foxholes we
were hardly ready for a ground or mortar attack. Several minutes
later the situation deteriorated even further.

A man from our platoon got up to walk toward the CO's
position. On his way he accidentally tripped the wire leading to
someone's flare. There was a sudden shot, and he fell to the

ground. Men rushed to his aid from all directions. They sat him up and began tending his arm while someone radioed for a medical chopper.

In a few minutes a Huey hovered overhead with its spotlight glowing on the landing zone below. A short time later our wounded man was on his way back to Chu Lai. I never saw him again. I knew that he could be badly hurt, but like a lot of other men, I envied him. It was no joy taking a bullet, I was sure but for him the war was probably over. In a few weeks he'd leave a hospital in Japan and be on his way home. That bullet, although painful, was a blessing. It may have saved his life. It was a trade most men in the field would gladly have made.

The following day we continued our journey northward. After humping until mid-morning we stopped for a rest near a clump of trees. On a hill a few yards above us was a small hootch. Some of the men wanted to search it immediately for sign of the VC or NVA, including me.

"I want to go up there," I told Edwards. It was a foolish notion, but I wanted to make something useful out of the whole crazy expedition. I was also beginning to feel that frustration that came with humping and digging foxholes. To put it simply, I wanted to get into the action.

"You stay down here," said Edwards. "We've done this before."

Fine, I thought. Go up there and get your ass blown off.

The hootch was filled with rice, they reported, and in a few minutes they had it burning vigorously.

Suddenly the skies opened up, and in a minute or two we were soaking wet. We stood there without any shelter for a long time, finally heading for a clump of trees nearby. It didn't do much good. The cold, soaking rain continued for about half an hour, making us miserable.

As I stood there I felt my leg itching. I rolled up my fatigue pants and discovered a hole in my leg. It was a round, red circle, and a single drop of blood was making its way toward my rain-soaked sock. I became slightly elated over the possibility that I had been shot. It was my ticket home: a painless, harmless, little wound, provided by an NVA sniper. But Edwards took a look and came to the conclusion that I had been bitten by a leech. They were wiggling all over the wet grass at my feet like night crawlers. It was a disappointment, and knowing that a leech had been riding with me for hours didn't help. It sucked my blood as I humped along, finally dropping back to earth when it became too heavy to hang on.

The rain finally stopped, and we were ordered to set up a perimeter on a nearby hill. It was close to dark, and there were claymores to set and foxholes to be dug. A few of the men in the platoon got out of that detail by volunteering to set up an ambush site along the trail behind us. The rest of us set about our work.

As the sun was drifting over the Laotian horizon, there was a burst M-16 fire from the ambush site. We headed for our weapons, anticipating action. But it was a false alarm. Two civilians, a woman and a child, had wandered into the area and been shot. Now the platoon sergeant was scrambling back to the company area to get a medical chopper. It would be up to the doctors in Chu Lai to correct the mistake our men had made.

As we set up that night, one of the men in our platoon suffered a severe burn when he accidentally tripped one of his own flares. Trip flares were intensively hot, and it didn't take much contact to do damage. He sat up all night with his blackened hand. They had told him it was too late to call in another chopper, and that he'd have to hold out until morning. He spent the next eight hours in terrible pain, but he managed to hang on until his rescue ship showed up at dawn. We stood by enviously as the chopper lifted off.

The rather somber mood that had hovered over the company changed quickly when we were told that the mission was about to end. We were heading south again, back to the comforts of Karen. I remember thinking how lucky we had been to have avoided the horror of a nighttime ambush or mortar attack. We seemed so vulnerable, so open. But the enemy apparently hadn't been ready for us, and we slipped in and out before he could decide on a course of action.

There were to be no stops that day, except for a few brief rest periods, until we reached the end of the trail near Karen. The jungle, much thicker here than across the river, was again hot enough to bake our hides mercilessly. But we pushed on. During one of the rest periods a colonel, apparently the brigade commander, landed in a chopper about a quarter of a mile behind me. Although I never saw him I was told that he had fallen into the ranks and was humping along with us. I couldn't believe that a colonel would do such a thing.

His presence, though, gave me a new burst of energy. I figured that he must be twice my age and maybe overweight besides. But he was out there with his men, and I was impressed. It was comforting to have such a gritty CO so close by.

Around 4:00 P.M. we were almost within the shadow of Karen. We sat down under some trees to rest. The company, by then, was spread over a quarter of a mile down the trail.

The shade of the trees felt icy cold. All we lacked was water. About five minutes earlier, we had passed a small well next to an abandoned hootch. The water in the well was milky white, and a dead frog floated spread-eagle on the surface. Despite our thirst, we walked on, not wanting the foul water to tear up our intestine.

But the need for water soon overcame the fear we had of getting dysentery. Someone suggested that we return to the well, and in a minute some of the men were busy gathering canteens for the trip back. I didn't have the stomach to go with them. But when they returned, I drank as much as I could from my canteen without breathing in the stench. I tried not to think about the slimy texture and the sickening color. I felt good, for the moment. My thirst was gone.

The company began moving again in 30 minutes. We passed a group of ARVNs heading in the opposite direction, apparently to secure the area we had just left. They had killed a big, wild boar, and they were carting it up the trail on a pole. It had just been gutted, and blood was dripping from the carcass. The ARVNs, most of them obviously in their teens, giggled and chattered with embarrassment as they went by.

It was good to see Vietnamese soldiers going out to secure Vietnamese ground, but I was convinced that this ragged band would soon disintegrate in the face of an NVA attack. They looked like children, too young to understand how dangerous their mission might be. Maybe, I thought, it was better that way.

When dusk approached we learned that our platoon had been chosen to set up an ambush along the trail that night. The rest of the company was going back to Karen. We moved back down the trail about 50 yards and set up a pair of claymores facing north. A guard order was hastily arranged, and we settled in for the night.

I was called about 3:00 A.M. One man was awake at all times, while the rest of the platoon slept. If someone approached, he had to detonate the claymores and make sure that everyone knew which way to fire. I sat on my rucksack, just about six feet off the trail. There was a bright moon overhead, and the trail was visible for approximately 50 feet. After that, it disappeared into over-hanging trees and shrubs.

The rest of the men were scattered on either side of the trail, sleeping peacefully on their rucksacks. The detonator lay at my feet. If I saw someone coming down the trail, no matter who it was, I simply had to squeeze the detonator and blow him away. Shoot first, and ask questions later. No one had any business on that trail after dark, and everyone knew it, including the civilians. Only the VC and NVA moved at night, and then at their own risk. Those were the rules of the game.

For two hours I sat and watched. Nothing moved. I prayed that no one would appear on the trail. I really don't know what I would have done. In self-defense, and out of fear, I probably would have detonated the claymores, but it wouldn't have been easy. I didn't want to kill anyone, innocent or otherwise. Still, I wanted even less to die myself. I just wasn't ready to decide the life-and-death issue.

But there I was, possibly responsible for the lives of an entire American platoon, and still undecided about what I would do. It was lunacy. Total lunacy. How could either side win with people like me sitting at the trigger? Someone like Edwards should have been there in my place. He seemed to enjoy killing and he didn't hesitate to shoot. He obeyed orders without question. With 500,000 men like him, maybe the war might edge closer to a victory than a stalemate. He was the kind of soldier that a nasty little war like Vietnam required. He didn't let his brain and his sense of duty get jumbled together. He was efficient and effective. In the eyes of the military, I thought, Edwards was an excellent soldier.

When my two hours finally expired I woke my replacement and told him where to find the claymore detonator. He nodded, and I was asleep in less than five minutes.

In the morning we returned to Karen and the comforts of our elevated perimeter. We didn't know it at the time, but our field mission was about to end. Already the artillery boys were breaking down and getting ready to move.

The last days on Karen passed quickly. The inevitable case of dysentery from the bad water came and ran its course, loosening me up for about a week. Several times each day I took my shovel and headed for the semi-privacy of a dirt pile near our bunker to relieve myself. I suppose I should have gone to the medic, but aside from an upset stomach, it was little more than an inconvenience.

The day finally came—around August 1—for the final evacuation of Karen. Everything went that day—artillery, hootches, tools— even the berms that once guarded the artillery pieces were leveled. All that remained at nightfall was a handful of GIs, including me. The evacuation had been cut short by a heavy rain and a thick, white fog, stranding our squad for the night. We huddled under a handful of culverts, watching for signs of the enemy, even though visibility was barely 20 feet. Flares were shot from a mortar outfit a few hundred yards away and floated lazily overhead, providing some assurance that we hadn't been forgotten. But we were clearly alone on that hill, maybe a dozen of us, and I was hoping that the enemy didn't know it. If an attack came, we'd be sitting ducks.

As if the situation wasn't bad enough, I began to get sick, not with diarrhea, but with something much more subtle. During my stretch of guard I found it impossible to stay awake. After a few minutes of staring out through the end of the culvert, I drifted to sleep. Someone woke me, but in a few minutes it happened again. No matter how hard I fought, I couldn't stay awake. At the same time I was cold and slightly dizzy. Something was affecting me, but I couldn't do anything about it. I was even too weak and helpless to be embarrassed when someone woke me for the third time. Fortunately, he didn't make an issue of something that I considered to be very serious. I pictured myself being court-martialed, or even shot, but there was nothing I could do.

Mercifully, the night brought no attack. We packed up our mud-covered gear and waited for a chopper. In a few minutes we were sitting with the rest of D Company on another hill, waiting for headquarters to move us. My platoon gathered around a bunker, and I laid down on a nearby pallet and drifted to sleep. Several hours later, I woke up with a sharp pain. I pulled a blood-swollen tick from my back and another from my groin. I was still weak and light-headed, and still unaware of the nature of my illness.

The next morning a Chinook landed nearby, and we gathered in its belly for a ride to another firebase. Just as the big chopper was about to take off, our platoon sergeant scurried aboard and shouted something. He held up his M-16 and showed the butt. It had been shattered by a sniper's bullet a second earlier. The NVA, I thought, were closing in one day too late.

It was such a great relief to be going back to a rear firebase. I didn't know how much, though, until I scrambled off the Chinook. We had landed in the same area where our journey westward had begun one month earlier. The firebase was small, not much bigger than Karen. But the few strands of electric wire, the bustle of Vietnamese civilians along Highway 1, and the abundance of men in clean uniforms convinced me that we were once again in the midst of civilization.

I dropped my gear and rifle at a bunker along the perimeter. It was a spacious bunker, complete with a metal roof and a plywood floor, much like the bunkers in Ben Hoa. It was another sign that things were getting better.

Mike McMillan joined me a few minutes later. Mac, like me, was finishing his first couple of months in D Company. He was rather short, and his jet-black hair stood straight up. His face was round and fair. He almost looked Oriental. He was sensitive, too, and he had a good sense of humor. To me, he was the brightest spot in the second platoon.

Mac had one advantage over me. He hadn't antagonized anyone yet. He didn't smoke pot and seldom drank beer, so he wasn't a part of any clique. I suspected that he didn't care much for the Army or Vietnam. Still, he obeyed orders and showed more cooperation than any man in the platoon. He told me later that he was going to follow the program quietly until he got back home. It seemed like a sensible approach, and I envied his low profile, privately regretting that I hadn't managed to control my temper up on Karen.

After securing our gear, Mac and I picked up our rifles and headed for the main gate. There, a boy about ten was selling cans of Coke for 50 cents each, every one of them ice cold. We popped the tops and drank them down. I could never remember being more satisfied with a soft drink in my life.

We wandered back to the platoon's area along the perimeter, still caked with mud from our last night on Karen, and found several men rummaging through a brown mailbag. Mac and I finally got our chance, and I began to stack my treasures to one side: cookies from my mother, several letters, and two or three issues of my hometown newspaper, the *Oconomowoc Enterprise.*

I focused my attention on the letters first, but something caught my eye as I knelt in front of that dusty bag. On the front page of one of the Enterprises was a picture of a man in uniform.

I knew it could only mean one thing: somebody from Oconomowoc had bee killed in Vietnam. I sat and stared in disbelief. It was David Price.

The impact of what I had just seen didn't hit me right away. I picked up the mail and carried it slowly back to the bunker. Mac was already sitting on some sandbags nearby, hovering over a letter from his wife.

"What's the matter?" he asked

"A buddy of mine was just killed." I replied numbly. "He was with the Ninth Division."

Mac didn't say anything. He didn't have to. He knew how I felt. I walked to the side of the bunker and stared at the rice paddies and tree line in the distance. All I could see, though, was David shaking my hand as we parted back in Ben Hoa.

He seemed so alive, so elated over the fact that we had met one more time before we headed for the field. I could still see his face and his rumpled uniform. Dave never cared much for looking fashionable. He was too casual to care about such things. And his innocence returned to haunt me. Someone who thought he understood the war, like me, would be a more appropriate casualty. I had at least begun to mold the whole picture into some kind of rationalization; I thought I understood what was going on in Vietnam and why we were there.

But I was sure that David hadn't. He didn't seem to be interested in politics. He was just another draftee, someone responding without question to the judgment of his local board. It didn't matter if it was a "just" war, or an "unjust" war. He didn't ask questions. He loved his country and his community and his family too much to defy them. Now his devotion had cost him his life. I wanted to cry, but I couldn't. I guess I was still hoping that there had been some kind of mistake. The thought of David's death was too much to face. It was a concept that was too abstract. I slumped to the ground and found relief in a short nap.

We settled in for the night, with Mac pulling the first watch while I slept. But when he woke me I was in no condition to stand guard. I was soaking wet, not from the rain outside, but from my own sweat. Even though I was wrapped in a poncho and a blanket, I shook as though I had just finished a cold swim. Mac wanted to go for the medic, but I said I'd be all right if he'd just pull my guard, which he did. I fell back to sleep.

In my discomfort and near delirium my brain went wild. I was a little kid again, haunted by imaginary monsters dancing through my dreams. They scrambled around my head, robbing me of my rest. Relief came only with the warmest of the morning sun.

I couldn't eat breakfast because I had suddenly become nauseous. It felt good, though, to just sit and let the sun beat on my back. I was bone tired, even after ten hours of sleep, and Mac finally insisted that I see the medic. I walked across the firebase, and soon I was perched on a chair with a thermometer in my mouth. I felt incredibly light-headed, almost intoxicated.

"What's wrong with me?" I asked.

"You've probably got malaria," the medic said, nonchalantly. "You'll have to go back to Chu Lai to the hospital."

At first I didn't grasp what he was saying. My head was feather light. It was as though I had taken a dozen Darvon. I was floating painlessly.

"Nothing's going back for awhile," he said, yanking the thermometer. "You'll have to wait until tomorrow."

I nodded and left, not even bothering to ask what my temperature was. I headed back to the bunker and gave Mike the diagnosis. He rushed over to wrap me in a blanket and ordered me to sit down and rest, but I assured him that the misery of the previous night had passed. The only problem was my lack of appetite. I couldn't even look at a C-ration can. I sat for the next few hours in the sun, slowly regaining my strength.

That night I found myself standing in front of the platoon sergeant and hearing his call for volunteers for a bridge ambush. For some reason my hand went up. The sergeant, seeing me in the medic's tent earlier in the day, ignored me. When he had gathered his volunteers he broke from the group and began packing his gear.

"Sergeant, I want to go on the ambush," I said.

"You're sick. You stay here," he replied, not bothering to look up.

"There's nothing wrong with me," I pleaded. "I just have a touch of the flu. Look, I really want to go."

"All right. Pack up and be at the gate in five minutes."

I hurried back to the bunker and told Mac that I was joining him and the other men. He told me that I was crazy not to stay in camp, but I wasn't listening.

I didn't know why I wanted to go. Maybe I was looking for revenge for David's death. Or maybe I had something to prove. I wanted badly to win the approval of the rest of the men in D Company. I wanted them to know that I was gutsy and willing to take on the most dangerous assignments. I wanted to prove that I could be a good soldier, not one of the lame and lazy back in camp.

Around 15 of us climbed into a deuce-and-a-half and headed south about two miles. We were soon settling up near a small, one-lane metal bridge crossing a lazy river. The sun was just going down, and a handful of ARVNs were laughing and shooting at fish from the bridge. They were typical ARVNs: unkempt and unprofessional, too busy with their American-made toys to take the war seriously. They were told to board the truck, and they quickly obeyed. In a minute it was traveling farther south.

I found a spot along the edge of the road and laid down to sleep until it was my turn for guard. In my hurry to join the ambush I had forgotten my poncho. All I had was a blanket. I had the choice of either lying on it or under it, and since I was feeling the chills returning, I chose the latter. After an hour or so I was awakened by a number of painful little bites. I thought it was just mosquitoes, and I was too cold and drowsy to care. I lay there, trying to get as much rest as possible.

When Mac woke me for guard he offered to take my watch, but I refused. Across the road a second GI was on duty. We didn't speak to each other as I planted myself on a pile of sandbags next to the road. I felt tired and cold, but I was sure I could make it for my hour and a half.

It wasn't long, though, before I began to get the dry heaves. My stomach was jumping up and down in painful spasms. I had eaten nothing for supper, and there was nothing to throw up to give me relief. The man across the road just looked at me as I bent over every few seconds. Finally he asked if I was okay, and I nodded weakly. The heaves eventually left me, and I passed the rest of the watch in a kind of half daze. At 3:00 P.M. I woke my replacement and settled back under my blanket for a couple more hours of sleep.

Around 7:00 A.M. I awoke to voices on the bridge just a few yards away. It was the rest of the platoon, everyone except Mac and me. He was sitting next to me cleaning his M-16.

"You feel alright," he asked.

"I'm okay. I just feel woozy."

I sat up next to the road and soon discovered why I had been feeling painful bites through the night. I had accidentally lain down over a tiny anthill. Little red ants were scurrying in all direction. Somehow, though, I didn't care. I was nearly delirious and sick to my stomach again. I sat with my head in my lap, and my hands resting on my knees in front of me. Flies were eating on the open "gook sores" on my knuckles, but there wasn't much I could do about it. I swatted at them a couple of times, and then tried to ignore them. I felt like I was dead, a piece of decaying flesh.

The men on the bridge were laughing loudly at a GI named Mitchell, who was apparently providing some impromptu entertainment. He and I had never talked much before. He was just another face in the platoon. Suddenly he looked over at me and said something to his little audience. The rest of the men looked toward me as well, and then broke into laughter.

At that instant I hated all of them. I knew I had made a mistake not staying back at the firebase.

We all rode back on the truck that morning around 9:00 A.M. An hour later I was on a jeep heading south toward Chu Lai. There I was directed to the hospital, and eventually to a large bay where men with malaria were being treated. A nurse behind the counter, a blond about 25, told me to get dressed in pajamas and find a vacant bed. I felt very out of place, still wearing my coat of mud from Karen.

"Can't I at least take a shower?" I asked, smiling with embarrassment.

"You really ought to get dressed. Your temperature is 103."

I slipped into the light blue pajamas and was escorted to a bed at the far end of the bay. My attendant was a specialist 6 by the name of Martin. He was big, built like a football lineman, and he was all business.

"You better take a cold shower right away," he warned. "You've got to try and get that fever down."

In a few minutes I was standing under what seemed like ice-cold water. I endured it for as long as I could. I dried off and headed back to my bed. In a few minutes, I had drifted off to sleep.

It wasn't long, however, before Martin was shaking me. I rolled over on my back, feeling slightly delirious. All I wanted to do was sleep. Martin plunged a thermometer into my mouth, and I closed my eyes again to rest. When he took it out he had bad news.

"It's 105.6," he said. "You've got to get on the ice-bed. Come on. Get up."

I responded, but very slowly. He helped support me as I made my way down the aisle toward the reception desk. Just before we got there he ordered me to turn left.

"Get your pajamas off," he said.

I couldn't help but protest.

"I'm freezing," I told him.

"Get 'em off," Martin insisted. "Then lay down there."

He pointed to a bed with a dark green, rubber mat covering it. It had a funny, coiled pattern that reminded me of the back of my grandmother's old refrigerator.

I slowly stripped off my clothes and lay down. The rubber mat was extremely cold. Later someone told me it was kept at a constant 46 degrees. Martin laid a towel over my middle, and then turned to mix something. It had the ring of ice cubes hitting the sides of a big metal dish. Soon he turned back with a towel, soaking wet, and began applying it to my exposed chest and legs.

"What's that?" I asked, still unable to believe what was happening to me.

"It's a combination of ice water and alcohol," said Martin, still sober-faced. "It'll break your fever."

"What if I get pneumonia?" I said.

"That's a chance we have to take. It's happened before. We'll cross that bridge when we get to it. For now we want to make sure you don't die from malaria."

I tried to think about something besides the cold and the pain in my legs that came with the constant trembling, but I couldn't. There was a big clock on the wall that I kept watching as the second hand made its rounds laboriously. On the table next to me was a thermometer, and I checked my temperature every five or ten minutes, hoping desperately for some change.

Martin and a nurse soaked me down every few minutes, then left me to my wretched trembling. I looked down just once, and saw that my legs had turned blue. I was sure the exposure to the cold would kill me sooner than the malaria. The minutes passed slowly. Every time I picked up the thermometer I prayed that the misery of the ice water solution had begun to pay off. I began to wonder if I would have to spend the night there. I speculated over my chances to survive several more hours on the rubber mat.

Relief finally came. I was exhausted when the fever broke after nearly two hours. Martin checked the thermometer and told me that I was free to return to my bed.

"Can you walk?" he asked.

"Of course I can walk," I told him indignantly.

My legs ached badly as I reached down to put on my pajama bottoms. After slipping on my top I tried unsuccessfully to stand. Martin didn't say a word. He just grabbed my arm and helped me walk slowly back to bed.

"You let me know if that fever goes back up again," he said, handing me the thermometer.

I nodded. I had never been through such an ordeal in my life. I was grateful to be alive.

"I have malaria, right?" I said.

"Don't know," said Martin. "We have to check your blood to see what's wrong. It probably is malaria. But we have to catch it when it's active before we can start treatment."

It wasn't long before the nurse was standing over my bed, drawing a sample of blood. She said they needed samples three times a day, because malaria had a tendency to run in 48-hour cycles.

"Does that mean I'll be on the ice-bed again day after tomorrow?"

"Maybe. At least it's likely that your fever will try to go up again then."

The next day I rested comfortably. My biggest chore was penning a letter to my parents explaining my predicament. At first I thought about hiding the fact that I was in the hospital. Why shouldn't I keep them thinking I was still with the company? Did I have to put them through the trauma of knowing that I was fighting malaria?

I decided to make something up. I had to let them know I was in the hospital, I figured, or my mail would go to D Company for several weeks. I had to tell where I was, but what would scare them less than malaria?

I wrote in the first paragraph that I had the flu, just a minor case of dysentery and an upset stomach. The doctors, I said, just wanted me to rest for a few days. My problem was common, but harmless. I said I was enjoying my nights out of the rain, and that it was nice to be sleeping on sheets again.

I was sure I'd beat the malaria, and while I did, there was no sense in making everyone back home sick with worry. Let them think that things were going well. Hospital time was "good time." My 365 days were passing with regularity, and above all, I was safe.

My third day in Chu Lai was like my first. I showered three times, and lay on my bed with icepacks under my arms, until I had no choice but to return to the ice-bed. But I thought I did. Martin summoned me to the chilly mat after noticing that the ice packs and the showers hadn't done any good. My temperature was hovering around 103.

"Let's go. Get on the ice-bed," he told me.

"Not me. I'm not going to lay on that damn thing again."

"You don't have any choice. You want to die?"

I finally rose from the bed and followed him down the aisle. We started the ice water routine all over, and once again, I watched the red, second hand make its laborious rounds for two full hours.

On the fourth day I felt much better. I even drank a beer that someone had smuggled from the bar down the road. But on the fifth day the fever began to creep back on schedule. I showered a couple of times, and drank ginger ale, apple juice, and orange juice until I couldn't stand to look at them anymore, all to no avail. The fever persisted, and I knew that a trip to the ice-bed was inevitable. I dutifully went to the nurse at the front desk and told her that I was ready for another round with the Eskimo bath. She agreed, and back I went.

The sixth day brought me renewed hope that the fever was gone for good. The nurse had been taking her three daily blood samples, and I was sure that after nearly a week of searching the malaria bug would soon be isolated.

But I was wrong. On the seventh day the fever returned, and I found myself trying to digest my lunch on the ice-bed. I hovered around 103 for awhile, and then shot up to 104. That was in spite of the ice water and alcohol, and the towels, and the 46-degree mat. I remembered then that malaria had killed GIs before, and I was swept with fear. There was one particular type, *falsiparum*, that was more serious than the other type, and I was sure that I had it.

For the first time since coming to the hospital I thought seriously about dying. I lay there for a few minutes, trying to decide what to do. People who are dying usually have their relatives summoned for a final goodbye. That was impossible, of course. But I imagined my parents standing over me, staring down with rather inevitable looks. They knew I was dying, but they didn't say anything. Their presence, at least, was comforting. They had managed to accept the fact that their son was dying. I folded my hands over my chest and began to pray. I felt embarrassed going to God, because I had never needed him before. But it was my last hope. I was sure he was listening as I passed along my message.

"If this is your will. Lord, I'm ready to die," I said.

Suddenly Martin was standing over me. For the first time he wore something besides his business expression. He looked genuinely concerned.

"You'd better relax, I'm tell you," he admonished. "You're making it awfully tough on yourself."

I nodded, and folded my hands again. In less than 30 minutes the fever had broken. I sat up relieved, and returned to my bed. I was grateful, and somewhat puzzled, at my reprieve from death.

On the eighth day *falsiparum* malaria was the diagnosis. I began receiving little purple pills in a paper cup each day. There was no more ice-bed and no more blood samples. I was weak, but very relieved. All I wanted to do was enjoy the clean sheets and get as much sleep as possible.

On the morning of the tenth day, just as I began to develop a new pattern for laziness, a specialist 4 came up to my bed, looked at my chart, and ordered me to get up. He said I was due to be shipped south to Cam Ranh Bay for a period of recuperation. We went by truck to the airport in Chu Lai, and from there we flew directly to Cam Ranh Bay. I remember the people in the plane rather vividly; GIs with superficial wounds, and civilians on stretchers with I.V. tubes dangling above them.

As usual, I dozed off to sleep as soon as the plane left the ground.

Ten days in the hospital, and ten days in Cam Ranh Bay. That was the usual schedule for men with malaria. For me, it meant another week and a half away from the field, and I was beginning to enjoy it more and more. Cam Ranh Bay was especially attractive because it was isolated from the rest of the war. At least it seemed that way. The recuperation area was located along the beautiful beaches of the South China Sea. The area was full of the things I took for granted back home: paved roads, traffic, an outdoor theater, a PX with a tiled floor, and even mobile homes for the nurses and VIPs. It was a busy place, with no flack jackets or M-16s.

I was taken directly to a little metal building, one of a half dozen standing in a neat row just a hundred feet from the water. There were rows of beds on either side of the bay. A few of the others were also recovering from malaria, but there were also men with broken limbs, bullet wounds, infections, and assorted illnesses. Everyone was dressed the same light blue pajamas and white slippers.

Except for the cinder track that ran round the buildings, and the dirt road that led out of the compound, the area was covered with sand. It was deep, so deep that walking on it for even a few seconds became uncomfortable, even painful. To overcome that problem the Army had installed wooden sidewalks that led every- where, even to the latrine, which was the finest I had seen in Vietnam since I arrived. It has a cement floor and over a dozen flush toilets.

I remember the latrine vividly because I was sitting there one afternoon with a piece of the sports section from the _Stars and Stripes_ when an old mamsan walked in. She was carrying a broom, and she began to sweep around the stools. When she came to one that was occupied, she tapped the man on the leg until he raised his feet so the she could sweep underneath. When it was my turn I did the same thing. It was a unique experience, but it bothered me a lot less that I thought it would.

The days in Cam Ranh Bay went by quickly. Fortunately, my family and friends kept me occupied with mail. There wasn't a single day when I didn't receive at least one letter. There were also boxes of cookies, newspapers, and even magazines. As usual, I read my letters several times before I threw them out. I spent most of my free time on my bunk, writing return letters and enjoying the cool breeze off the nearby water. I urged my family to keep up its support, and apologized more than once for writing slightly illegible letters.

I expected to spend my ten days lounging on the beach,

pampered by the camp personnel, but I was wrong. They woke us at 6:00 A.M. for calisthenics, then forced us to run a full lap around the cinder track before we got breakfast. We usually spent the morning filling sandbags and · stacking them around the hootches. It was difficult to stand in the sun after a bout with malaria, but the NCOs didn't push very hard. A lot of them were recovering too, and they were sympathetic. We took numerous and lengthy breaks.

We had the afternoons off if we worked in the morning, but our opportunity for activity was limited. I spent most of my time, and money, eating chocolate shakes and sitting next to the big fan in the mess hall, which also served as a restaurant between meals.

At night, unless it rained, movies were shown outdoors. There was plenty of beer and soda, and ample bleacher space. The air was always filled with music, rock music from the states, blaring over the camp loudspeaker system.

I got used to the casual routine, and I dreaded the day when I'd have to return to D Company and life in the field.

ഇ

Leaving Cam Ranh Bay was like being drafted all over again. The feel of not wearing a uniform was comfortable and refreshing, and I hated to give it up.

I flew back to Chu Lai and found that the battalion had stationed itself there temporarily for operations west of the city. The company area was pretty bleak, just a row of canvas hootches a hundred yards off the road. The company first sergeant, who looked more like a gym teacher than a career NCO, found a bunk for me in a hootch a few yards from the company's headquarters. It was a dark, eerie place. The flaps had been pulled down on both sides. Just a trickle of light filtered through the dirty screen doors on either end. There were two men inside, eyeing me nervously as I looked for a vacant bunk. Neither of them spoke, and I stayed for just a few seconds. I was sure they were pot-heads, waiting for the coast to clear so they could light up again, and I didn't want to get in their way. I decided that I'd sleep in the hootch and nothing more.

I went back to the company area and asked a clerk for my rucksack, the one with the shrapnel holes. I remembered that it still contained stationery and envelopes, and I thought I'd write a few final letters before going back to the field.

But the rucksack was nowhere in sight. Finally someone told me to look through the storage tent, and I found it in the corner, empty. When I protested to the clerk he just shrugged. It was nobody's fault but my own. I told myself. Never trust a RAMF. That was a basic rule for a grunt. There were more thieves in the rear than honest men. I lost my paper and envelopes only because I was too stupid to take them with me. I swore I'd never let it happen again.

That night my foot began to itch terribly. It actually started to bother me back in the hospital in Chu Lai. After every shower the itching on my left arch flared up, and by the time I got to Cam Ranh Bay I had developed a red lump about the size of a half dollar. It had a rough edge and a soft, watery middle, kind of like a gook sore, but I couldn't stop scratching it. Whenever I touched it, though, the skin would break and a clear, slimy liquid would suddenly appear.

The next morning, after noticing that my foot was beginning to swell, I asked to see a doctor at the hospital, and the first sergeant reluctantly agreed to let me go for the morning.

The diagnosis came quickly. I had ringworm, with a possible infection. The doctor signed a profile for me and made some notes on my medical papers. I tucked them neatly into a folder and headed back to the company area. The doctor had given me some penicillin pills and ordered me to return in a week.

The first sergeant wasn't very happy about the profile, but there was nothing he could do. He found some light duty for me once in awhile, but I was generally relegated to nightly guard duty on a bunker near the battalion area. It wasn't much responsibility, though. The bunker was hundreds of yards from the Chu Lai perimeter, far from any potential action. We just went through the motions, usually sleeping until the duty sergeant made his nightly rounds around 3:00 A.M. and woke us. He'd give us a gently warning to stay awake, and then leave. In a few minutes we'd be sleeping again.

Just a few days before I was scheduled to see the doctor I overheard the first sergeant and the clerk talking about some-thing that had happened in the field. I stood outside the tent for a minute, listening to bits of the conversation.

"Tanner got hit when he put Mitchell on the chopper..."

"Maybe we should put him in for the silver star, not the bronze..."

The company clerk walked out a minute later, and turned toward the supply tent.

"What's that all about?" I asked.

"The recon platoon got wiped out," he said. "Thirteen killed and 26 wounded. The platoon got hit, too. Mitchell and Williams are dead. Tanner took a bullet in the leg. He's in the hospital."

I couldn't believe my ears. It was by far the worst day in the field for the battalion since I came to Vietnam. A man died every now and then in the field, but 15 at once, and two men from my own platoon? The VC, not very well armed or organized, at least from what I had seen, were capable of inflicting casualties on the Army, but not like this. It had to be an NVA force, a substantial one, to wipe out so many men. I was shocked to learn that such a disaster could take place. We had the jets and the artillery, and by far the largest force of men. But somehow all that had meant nothing to the recon platoon. Out of less than 45 men, barely a half dozen had managed to escape without injury.

I limped away from the company area and sat on a pile of sandbags, staring at the mountains to the west. I pondered, once again, about the probability that I would also die in Vietnam before my twelve months expired.

Later the brigade doctor gave me another profile, but it was good for just a few days. When it expired I reported to the first sergeant and told him my status. But I also told him about my left foot, now swollen to twice its size. Despite the penicillin pills, and the rest, the redness and the swelling had increased noticeably.

Just the sight of that foot bought me more time in the rear. No one even bothered to ask to see my profile. They just assumed that I was too disabled to be humping with a rucksack in the field.

I made a third trip to the doctor, and he outfitted me with crutches, which I took without hesitation. They were the perfect symbol of my unfitness for field duty. As long as I held onto them, I figured there was no need to worry about going back to hump with the company.

As I left the hospital I remembered that Carlson was in a small medical installation just down the road. I hitched a ride and went in to see him.

He was sitting on the edge of his cot, staring straight ahead and puffing anxiously on a cigarette. We shook hands, and he was glad to see me, but there was obviously something else on his mind. In a minute he was telling me what had happened in the field.

Mitchell had been killed when a sniper opened up on the platoon as it crossed a small river. He took a round in the lung, and his buddies helped him to safety as he gasped his final breath. Carlson thought he might have lived if someone had discovered the hole and plugged it, but everyone was too busy avoiding the sniper's fire.

While the platoon was pinned down, Tanner, not knowing that Mitchell was dead, picked him up and carried him to a waiting chopper. When he ran back to his position he took a bullet in the leg. At first he thought it was a mosquito bite, but in a few minutes the pain had become unbearable. A second chopper was called in, and Tanner was taken to a medical facility back in Chu Lai.

"He cried a little when they told him that Mitchell was dead," said Carlson, dragging on his second cigarette.

Williams, he said, died when he walked over a command-detonated landmine. He was walking just ahead of Carlson when they heard a loud click. Williams whirled around and stared, his eyes nearly popping out of his head. He knew what was happening, and he was stricken with fear. He was a dead man and he knew it. The mine, a 105 round with a wire running from it into the bushes nearby, exploded with incredible force. Carlson was hurled several yards by the impact. He had been standing 20 feet away, just out of range of the larger pieces of shrapnel. Still, his whole body was peppered with tiny specks of metal. He said the doctors once told him that it would take years for the fragments to work themselves free. For now, they were just a minor irritation.

"I'm going to run this thing as far as it'll go," said Carlson, holding up his profile. "I'm never going back to the field. I'll sham. I'll do every shit detail they want, but I'm not going back."

"I've never seen anything like it before," he went on. "Williams just disintegrated. All they found was a piece of his rib and a boot. They wrapped the remains in a plastic bag, and it sat on the chopper next to me when I was medevaced."

After a few minutes I got up to leave, shaking Carlson's hand and wishing him luck in his attempts to stay out of the field.

ᏣᏛ

It wasn't long before the company headquarters was moved back to Duc Pho. We were apparently being sent closer to home during the upcoming rainy season. That was good news, particularly after the horror that swept the battalion in the field earlier in the month.

Back in Duc Pho, with a few days remaining on my latest profile, I pulled guard duty and sometimes joined the men working the morning garbage detail. But most of my time was spent in the supply tent with a sergeant who welcomed the assistance. He looked rough, and I guessed he was nearly 40. He was skinny, too, and a chain smoker. The word around the camp was that he was an alcoholic. We had a good relationship for several days. I stayed off other dirty details while I was in his tent, and he had someone to do much of his work. It also provided me with a chance to stay out of the rain, which meant a lot with the monsoons approaching. Already in October the rains came daily, and the bunkers and perimeter area were constantly flooded.

During the same time I was being treated with shots of penicillin, one on each side of my buttocks after breakfast. The shots were administered by a medic in the battalion area. The doctor was usually away. He came around once a day to check on the sick men in the battalion and decided whether or not to grant them additional time on their profiles.

He was probably under pressure to keep as many men in the field as he could. His patients, on the other hand, were usually arguing for more time.

It was a kind of pitiful battle. Men, too scared to go back to the field, pleaded their cases with a doctor afraid not to send them, even though he probably wouldn't hesitate to keep them home from work if they were his patients back in the states. The doctor, obviously uncomfortable with his non-medical pressures, usually acquiesced. If he gave them a couple more days to rest, what would it hurt? The war wasn't going anywhere. They'd eventually get back to the field, and even if they didn't, there were plenty of other men to do the fighting.

I remember how ironic it seemed at the time, grunts who looked down on the RAMFs were themselves pushing for extra time in the rear. It was hypocritical, but only men who were insane really wanted to be back in the field. Besides, it was a challenge trying to wriggle an extra day or two on a profile. It was akin to beating the RAMFs at their own game.

My foot, twice its normal size and red with infection, stuck out wherever I went. In the lunch line one day several men actually turned and stared. They had never seen anything like it. It was puffy and red and ugly, and the skin was stretched almost to the point of splitting. It was embarrassing, but I had no place to hide. There wasn't a boot big enough in Duc Pho to accommodate me.

After about five days the penicillin began to take hold. My original problem, described as ringworm infection and _cellulitus_, began to fade. But the swelling remained above my ankle, even though I had no pain. It was actually the perfect profile. It provided me with no discomfort, but it was ugly enough to convince even a medic that something was still seriously wrong. No man could go to the field, I thought, with a leg that looked like that.

After another week I managed to slip on my boot, although I couldn't tie it. The medic gave me another seven days extension on my profile, which didn't make the first sergeant very happy. It meant that I would remain one of the ragged crew in the rear, sometimes described by the Army as the "sick, lame, and lazy." It was humiliating to some, but it was certainly safer than duty in the field. There probably wasn't a man in D Company that wouldn't have gladly traded his M-16 for twelve months on the garbage detail.

The calendar, after all, was the god of every GI. It made no deals, and it only made one promise. If a man could keep himself alive for twelve months, he could go home.

But life in the rear was frustrating. I finally tired of the profile game, and asked that I be allowed to join the company in the field. I expected some kind of praise for my courageous act, but there was none. The first sergeant didn't seem to care one way or the other. His indifference made me regret my foolish act. I felt as though I had betrayed myself, as though I had flown headlong into the face of common sense.

But it was too late. Arrangements were made for me to leave the next morning, and I was ordered to be on the chopper pad by 8:00 A.M.

There was an eerie quietness about the platoon when I got off the chopper that morning. The men were just settling down after apparently humping for several miles, and no one spoke a word. They seemed much older, dirtier, and quieter than the last time I had been with them.

Edwards was still there, and Mac, too. But there were a

surprising number of new faces, and they seemed to stick out
from the rest. Maybe it was their newer uniforms, or boots that
seemed shinier than the others. But there was something else,
too. They seemed so much younger than the veterans. Their eyes
were wider, and their faces seemed fresher. They were like boys,
mixed into a platoon of men. The death of Williams and Mitchell,
and the fear of being under fire, had taken their toll. I was sure
that my face also looked boyish and virgin. After all, I had been
safe in the rear when the platoon suffered its fatalities. I was sure
the veterans in the platoon were thinking about that when I
walked off that chopper, and it made me feel slightly conspicuous. I felt like the man who showed up at the job after the work
was done.

To my surprise, nothing was said about Williams or Mitchell.
It was as though they had never existed.

We spent the night there, and the next day we humped for
several miles before settling down for a rest near a little village.
Late that afternoon we saddled up and walked a couple of hundred
yards toward a clearing. We passed a mortar platoon heading in
the opposite direction, and one man caught my eye. He was
carrying the base for the .82 mm mortar on his back. His head
was bowed, and the sweat was shiny on his face. He looked up at
me as we passed, and I could see that he was miserable. Carrying
the base, which must have weighed 40 pounds or more, didn't
excuse him from carrying a rucksack, either. It was sandwiched
between the round metal object and his arched back.

Seeing him that afternoon made me realize that humping with
a couple dozen rounds of M-79 ammunition wasn't all that bad.
At least I could stand up straight.

After dropping our gear in a clearing, the second platoon
headed for the village, almost hidden in a gathering of trees.
There were half a dozen hootches, all empty, plus a few pigs in a
makeshift pen fashioned from tree branches. Baskets were
scattered everywhere, many of them half filled with rice. The VC,
or NVA, had apparently seen us coming and deserted the area
before we arrived.

We sat down in the shade after checking several bunkers and
one-man foxholes along the trail leading through the village.
There was no sign of the enemy any-where. Several of the men
began dumping the rice on the ground and mixing it with dirt.
Others pulled out their lighters and started the hootches on fire.
It was a routine operation, I knew, but it was the first real

"search and destroy" I had been involved in. The idea was to destroy everything that might be of use to the enemy. That made sense, and I had no objections.

But it was the way in which the second platoon killed the pigs that turned my stomach. I watched someone open the pen and free the frightened animals, while other men sat nearby and patiently carved sticks into sharp daggers. Then one of them walked over to one of the pigs and drove the stick into its side. It let out a squeal that raised goose bumps on my arms. Soon other men were joining the fun, racing after the pigs and jabbing them with their wooden daggers. The little animals ran between the trees and hootches, trying desperately to escape. The men were laughing loudly.

I jumped to my feet and looked at the platoon sergeant, hoping he would see my displeasure and call a halt to the ragged slaughter. But he just stared, defying me to do something. He must have thought that after the platoon lost two men earlier to the enemy, the sadistic assault on the pigs was good therapy for his men. He smoked a cigarette and watched impassively as the last pig was cornered and finally put to death.

The chase lasted for about five minutes. One of the pigs, weighing maybe 45 pounds, was hoisted to the top of a burning hootch. There he sat, spread-eagle at the tip of the roof, with a cigarette stuck in his mouth and an old Army cap cocked over one ear.

It was a ridiculous sight, and I couldn't help but laugh. But I immediately felt ashamed, fearing that some of the sadism in the other men was also in me. And I didn't have any excuse. I wasn't with the platoon when Williams and Mitchell were killed. I was in no position to judge their feelings. Maybe watching other GIs die would change everything for me, too. Maybe killing those dumb animals seemed justified to men who had been targets in a shooting gallery just a week before.

I tried to put the village incident out my mind as quickly as I could. I was almost to the point of giving up on making sense out of what was happening in Vietnam.

The night passed quietly. In the morning we were back inside a Chinook, heading for Duc Pho.

We stayed there a couple of days, resting in the battalion area. After that we took off on foot for a firebase about three miles to the north for a few nights of perimeter guard. The platoon's hike through the jungle and rice paddies was uneventful that day, except for the sighting of a skeleton just outside the firebase as we finished our short journey. The company, in single file, entered the firebase as the skull and bones lay just a few feet off the path. Most of the men just looked at the curious sight. But one man behind me, a friend of Edward's, couldn't resist the temptation. As we entered a church to escape a sudden shower, I turned and saw him carrying the skull under his right arm. He set the skull on the dirt floor next to him, and the two of them began searching for a name for their new friend. They were like kids with a Christmas toy, trying to get attention from the other men. In an hour or two they tired of the game and tossed the skull out the door.

That night, as we rested along the perimeter, Edwards informed me that I was going on KP the next morning. KP? Was he crazy? Infantrymen didn't pull KP, not in Vietnam. There had to be some mistake, or else it was just a bad joke. I told him to go to hell, but he insisted that I had to be in the mess hall by 5:00 A.M. He said he'd be back in the morning to get me.

"They've got to have somebody from our squad, and you're the man with the least time in country," he said, showing his nervous half-grin.

"Go to hell. I'm not pulling any KP."

To my surprise, he left, but in a minute he was back with the sergeant. Five minutes later I was in the mess hall, getting ready to serve breakfast. We finished up about nine. Only about two-dozen men went through the line. It was a slightly humiliating experience, and I knew that new the sergeant had every reason to think I was a troublemaker. My image had sunk to new depths.

We humped back to Duc Pho a day later. They sent the second platoon to a dirty, brown, ragged tent for the night. There we found a couple dozen cots, some good and some not so good, scattered helter-skelter inside. A few men hurried ahead to pick out the best bunks, as usual, but I was too proud. I went up to the latrine and read through some sports pages and relieved myself in leisure.

When I got back the cots were all taken. I had to dig one out of the supply room and set it up myself. I crammed it in between two others and headed up the road with Mac and two other men for a cold beer at the headquarters bar. It was a little, one-room hootch with a cement floor and open walls. There was a small bar and a few tables and chairs. Music from a tape recorder was playing loudly, cranking out soul music.

We set our M-16s in the corner and began pouring down 15-cent cans of Budweiser. We drank and talked for hours about life back in the states. We finally fumbled our way back to the platoon's tent and began to search for our cots. By then the rain had been coming down for hours, and I found my cot filled with water. I lifted one end to let the water drain, then laid down to sleep under my poncho.

Later, around 2:00 A.M., I woke up and realized that I was soaking wet. There was a hole in the tent that was dripping water near my feet, smack in the middle of the cot. The tent was so crowded that there was no place else to sleep. I emptied the cot again and fell back to sleep. I repeated the same process once more before morning.

We spent the next few days in the field, patrolling around Duc Pho and trying to stay dry, which was incredibly frustrating. The rain never seemed to stop, barely trickling to a drizzle during its kinder hours. I sat down every hour or so and took of my socks to try and wring them dry.

But keeping anything dry was impossible. Everything was saturated with water. I had nothing left in my rucksack or my pockets that escaped a drenching. It was impossible to keep my matches dry, so cigarettes were few and far between.

At night I'd pull my poncho over my head and curl up on my rucksack, trying to keep from touching the soft ground. The plastic poncho kept me warm, but it also left me soaking wet with my own sweat by morning.

After a couple of days we were turned back toward Duc Pho for a night in the old brown tent. Just knowing that we had a chance to get out of the rain boosted our morale.

For me, however, the return to Duc Pho was another letdown. The Vietnamese civilians had taken off for some kind of national holiday, and that left the mess hall without enough men to serve the battalion. That meant the GIs had to scrub the pots and pans, prepare the meals, clean the tables, and serve the food.

Somehow our platoon got tabbed for some of the manpower, and not surprisingly, Edwards came to me. He said I'd be on all day. I asked for him to split the shift so that I could prepare my gear for an expected trip to the field in the morning, but he refused.

I washed pots and pans for eight hours, my hands submerged

in hot soapy water the entire time. The "sink" was nothing more than a 55-gallon drum, split down the middle and set up on legs. By the end of the day I was exhausted, but grateful for one thing: the hot water and soap had completely cleaned away a troublesome sore on my right hand.

In the morning, as I put on my damp socks. I noticed that my feet were looking rather strange. The skin around my rain-soaked toes was peeling away, exposing pink skin underneath. There was no pain, but I suspected that something was seriously wrong. I requested the chance to go on sick call, which was reluctantly approved by the sergeant. Ten minutes later I was sitting in the medic's tent, watching another GI dab a liquid on the red sore just below his right knee. He had a rather anguished look on his face as he carefully nursed the open wound.

"What's that?" I asked

"I don't know, but I can't get rid of it."

I paused for minute, glancing back at my bare feet.

"Did you ever see anything like this?" I asked.

He hardly bothered to look up. "No, but if it's anything like this you'll never get rid of it."

The medic, a specialist 4, set me down in a chair and took a close look at the peeling toes.

"This is pretty bad," he said.

He rose to his feet and walked over to a table for some cotton.

"Do you think you'll have them off?" I joked.

"I hope not," he said, not cracking a smile.

He gave me some medicine and told me to apply it regularly, and to keep my feet as dry as possible.

What is it anyway, Doc?" I asked.

"Jungle rot," he replied.

ଔ

The platoon headed out to the boondocks that afternoon, leaving me behind with yet another profile. When they returned they talked about coming under fire as they walked along an abandoned railroad bed. The snipers hit them from the north and south, pinning them down for about an hour. They had desperately needed the grenade launcher, and I had been the last platoon grenadier. Two others were in the rear being treated for malaria.

Several men bubbled with the excitement of the encounter, but they were also disappointed that they hadn't been able to dislodge the snipers. A grenade launcher, they said, would have done the trick.

None of them was as disappointed as I was. I was the big loser, I thought. It was my weapon, after all, that might have turned a sniper incident into something glorious for the 2nd platoon. I could have been the hero. I felt like I had just let the winning touchdown slip through my fingers in the end zone as time ran out. I cursed by bad luck, feeling terribly frustrated. I was sure I would have had no qualms that day about shooting at the enemy. I would have been willing to kill to salvage my image in the platoon.

It wasn't long before I was back on a profile. My legs continued to swell up, so I ended up back in Duc Pho pulling duty in the company area.

But a few days later I was sent west to a firebase called "Cork" where the battalion had just opened some new operations. Cork was a god-forsaken place. It was nothing but a high hill scraped bare and peppered with makeshift bunkers. It was surrounded by other large hills, all covered with dense greenery. And it was a small base. A man could walk across it in 30 seconds.

Unlike other firebases I had seen, Cork was without a single wooden building. There was no mess hall, not even a tent. Most of the meals were provided by C-rations, except for the rare times when a chopper would bring in a hot meal. Cork was obviously a temporary setup, and I was sure I wouldn't be there long.

During the day I usually sat around in the bunkers, but occasionally the sergeant in charge of the profiles would have me on the "shit burning" detail. We'd carefully mix fuel oil in with the waste from the outhouses and then start a fire. It would create a ghastly black cloud of smoke, and a smell that kept the other men at the far end of the firebase. Every few minutes we'd take a board and still the soupy substance, pouring in more fuel oil and relighting it.

If there was one job in Vietnam that held no dignity, it was burning shit. It was unquestionable the bottom of the totem pole. Fortunately, I didn't do it very often. There were plenty of profiles on Cork to spread around that ignominious duty.

I expected to pass a few days of my tour up on Cork, and nothing more. I was sure I was going back to the field. It was just

a matter of time. I was convinced that I'd spend my entire tour in
D Company, maybe going alternately from profile to field duty
until my tour ended on June 6, 1969.

But an interesting thing happened one day as I lounged in the
grass, waiting for my morning assignment. I looked up to find a
tall thin GI standing over me. He was wearing new fatigues, and
he had a camera hanging around his neck.

"You going out with that company?" he asked, pointing to
some grunts who were packing up for a ride to the field.

"Nope. I'm just here on a profile."

"You looking for a job?" he asked

"What do you mean?"

"The information office down in Duc Pho needs some writers
and photographers. Why don't you go see if you can work there
permanently? It sure beats the field."

I agreed. But writing and picture-taking were out of my line.
Besides, the last thing my company was going to do was let me
out.

"I can't take pictures," I said, fishing for an excuse that would
make him go away.

"You can write, can't you?" he asked

"Sure. I even took some English courses back in college. I
guess I could write."

"Think about it, when you get back to Dun Pho. I used to be a
grunt, too, but the PIO is really hurtin' for men."

He turned and walked away, following after the company that
was packing to leave. All I could remember was that his name
was Brandel.

His sudden appearance at the firebase, and his offer of a
permanent job in the rear, haunted me for the rest of the day.
Was he just making conversation, or was there really a chance
that I could get out of the field for good? Maybe he was telling
everyone he saw about the opening. But then again, maybe permanent, trained replacements were on the way.

I was sure that Brandel's escape from the field was only a matter
of luck, a one-in-a-million chance that didn't happen by design.
It didn't seem logical that a specialized job like writer, or photographer, would go to a grunt in a line company. Yet, it had
happened to Brandel. Several times that day I dreamed that the

same luck might come my way, but each time I scolded myself for being so naive. There was no way I could get out of my last six months in the field. I tried desperately to forget that I had ever talked to Brandel.

I met two other interesting men during my short stay on Cork. One was a little Indian who had joined the Army after his tribe sold its reservation land in Washington State. He was a likeable guy, always smiling and full of stories about life on the reservation. He also had a few stories about his months in the field. One night, while we lay on our rubber mattresses just inside the perimeter, he told me about an incident in which his company took two VC suspects into custody. The company commander, a young lieutenant, told his men that they couldn't take the suspects along because they would slow down their operation. He said they would have to be executed.

My Indian friend, who was carrying an M-60 machine gun at the time, was one of three men to volunteer for a firing squad. They lined the suspects up next to a hootch, tied their hands to a bamboo pole, counted to three, and fired. The company then continued on its way.

My friend seemed to enjoy his tale. He was lying there on his mattress, smiling and watching the stars overhead as he recounted every detail. He seemed enormously satisfied. I stared at him for a few seconds, then rolled over and went to sleep.

Another infantryman that I ran across on Cork was a GI who had been with the recon platoon when it was ambushed a couple of months earlier. He was one of a half-dozen men, out of approximately 45, who survived the deadly encounter without a scratch. He remembered the day well.

The company was moving routinely along a rice paddy dike when the tree line burst open with enemy fire. He said there were more than 500 NVA soldiers bearing down on the platoon, and before the Americans could react, half of them were wiped out. It was just before dark, and that might have been all that saved him. He said he remembered crawling through the darkness with nothing more than a grenade in his hand, and no idea where his surviving comrades were hiding. He rested in the tall grass that night, and came upon an abandoned M-16 when he began to move with the coming daylight. He said he sat down to clean it, and while he was dusting it off he heard a noise behind him. He swung around and found an NVA in a full camouflage uniform, watching him and cradling an AK-47. He whirled the M-16 around and emptied a full clip at point blank range. The enemy soldier turned and began to walk away, but soon fell dead. The GI made his way back to another company.

Chapter 6
The Helter-Skelter War

The monsoons had a way of beating down a man's morale.
The world seemed forever wet and gray. Dense fogs came and
went, but always very slowly. And the moisture hung in the air
like it was suspended on a string. It was only a couple of months
earlier that the sun was shining and soft clouds were floating
overhead. Now the sun was gone, seemingly for good, and the
ground was black and spongy. Mud and water were inescapable,
no matter where we went or how hard we fought to stay clean and
dry.

Fighting the monsoons was pure futility. Even the most
determined man was finally overcome by the sheer length of the
rainstorms and the deep mud. With every step a man's boots
were sucked several inches into the ground, and the enemy now
became the weather, and there was no way to fight back. There
was nothing to do but bear it, and to do that it took as much
resolve as it did to pursue the VC in the jungle.

One morning we walked just about 50 yards from the Duc Pho
perimeter to destroy some earthen bunkers that may have been
used by the VC to launch their mortar attacks. I suppose they
could have been civilian bunkers, too, but we had no way of
telling. What surprised me was that they were so close to the
perimeter.

We packed them with C-4 and blew them away. It took about two hours, and toward nightfall we hiked another half-mile toward the south to set up an ambush in the middle of acres and acres of rice paddies. The land was flat, and there was no place to logically set up an ambush. But we formed a perimeter and sat down, pretending, at least, that we were an ambush. It was absurd, since the moon was rising and full, and visibility extended for a half-mile. That was the irony. If anything, we were a prime target for a mortar attack. Surely no VC or NVA, unless they were blind, would walk by a platoon of American GIs sitting in the middle of a rice paddy.

Because the ground was so saturated with water, we didn't bother to dig foxholes. We just covered ourselves with our ponchos and enjoyed a brief respite from the rains that had ceased an hour or so earlier.

For some reason I couldn't sleep. I pulled guard around midnight, and when I woke up my replacement, he said he was sick and wanted me to take his shift. I obliged. I finally fell asleep, but around 4:30 the word came around that we were moving out. At night? Were they crazy, I wondered?

We packed up and headed west just as the daylight began to filter through. But the morning also brought the rains once again, and it was coming down steadily as we put our weapons and gear over our head and waded through a river chest-deep. When we got to the other side the sergeant told us to sit and wait for further orders. The Army, typically, hadn't yet decided what to do with us yet.

The rain suddenly turned into a downpour, and I covered my head with my poncho and perched myself on my rucksack. The water was crashing down on me, but I was too exhausted to notice. I fell asleep as I sat there, and woke up an hour later when the platoon finally received its orders. We packed up and headed to a village just a couple of hundred yards away. The rain was still coming down incessantly.

The platoon, which appeared to be operating more and more without leadership, broke up into little groups and sought shelter in the hootches. They were better than most. They had cement floors and a well outside that had "1964" inscribed on its side. We figured some kind of overseas mission group had furnished the village with the well and the cement foundations.

I ducked into a hootch where an old man and woman were standing next to a fireplace. It was nothing more than a grass shack with woven mats for beds and crudely fashioned chairs. There were two other GIs and myself, and we all stripped to our shorts and hung our clothes next to the fire to dry. I borrowed a cigarette and sat back to enjoy it, relieved that I was out of the rain.

The old couple just stood off to the side, smiling. They finally helped hang up our clothes and offered us some water. In return we gave them some of our C-rations, which they seemed to welcome.

They were like all the other civilians we had run across in the field. I knew they were scared, and they had every reason to be afraid of us. God only knows what kind of horror stories had been circulated by the VC, or even by other civilians. Some were surely true. What intrigued me most about them was their smile. I wondered if they were just plain frightened, or if they were smiling out of contempt, just playing along until we left. Sometimes I even imagined that they were laughing at us, memorizing our conversations while pretending not to understand a word of English.

We offered the old man a cigarette, and he smoked it with enthusiasm. The old woman declined a cigarette, opting instead for a mouthful of beetlenut.

We sat in the hootch for about an hour, listening to the rain and enjoying dry cigarettes for the first time in several days. The fire felt good after so many days of humping in the cold rain.

Suddenly there was an explosion in the distance. It was hard to tell how far away it was, because of the rain, but it seemed to be just a couple hundred yards to the south.

Was it outgoing? Was it American artillery in the distance, or was the village being hit?

In a second there was another explosion, and then a third.

"Artillery!" said one of the men. We began to scramble back into our clothes, but the rounds began to come faster and closer. We were sure by then that the village was under attack. I grabbed my shirt and rucksack and threw them over my shoulder, taking my M-16 in my other hand, and rushed out the door. The other two men were right behind me.

We were joined outside by the rest of the platoon. Someone shouted that we were in the wrong place, that an assault was going to take place sometime soon, and that we were supposed to be the blocking force. Our position should have been on a hill a hundred yards to the north, not in the village.

Men scattered in all directions. Some dove into a Vietnamese bunker, including the sergeant. I ran for the hill with four other men, but when we got halfway there we heard a chopper overhead. It was bearing down on us, and there was no place to hide. It was an American chopper, of course, but to the pilot we were nothing but five men in green uniforms. We could be NVA or VC, as well as GIs.

Suddenly the chopper opened up, spitting rockets and mini-gun rounds. My heart fell. I dove for some bushes instinctively, knowing full well that they weren't going to protect me. The other men just ducked. We were all sure we were breathing our last breath.

But we got lucky. The guns fired over our heads toward a clearing beyond the village, and the chopper sailed harmlessly by. But one of the men in my group carried the radio, and he heard that a second assault chopper was following closely behind. He called in to tell them to stop it, but it was too late. The voice on the other end suggested that we find some cover.

We stood there for several seconds, trying to decide if we should run for the hill, taking the chance that we might be mistaken for fleeing NVA, or sit tight and hope the second ship was no less aware of us than the first. Then someone had an idea. Why not pop smoke grenades? There was no time to debate. The chopper came over the hill in an instant, and without hesitation we sent a cloud of blue, yellow, red and green smoke filtering skyward from our position. Again, the mini-guns opened up, followed by the rockets, and we stood frozen in our boots, praying that the rounds were going overhead. They did.

In a minute the whole operation had unfolded, and the sergeant emerged from his bunker with a handful of his pot-smoking buddies. They were laughing, like some kids who had just thrown stones at the schoolhouse windows. The sergeant, a 19-year-old instant NCO, had nearly gotten me killed, along with a lot of other men. Now he stood with his cronies, getting a kick out of the close call.

The five of us turned and walked up the hill, not bothering to wait for the rest of the platoon. I sat down and fell asleep once again as the rain stopped and the sun came out for the first time in a week.

That afternoon we drifted back toward a firebase called Liz, just south of Duc Pho. On the way we came upon a group of hootches, and to our surprise, found several men in black pajamas standing nearby. They were young, and their heads were shaved bare. We assumed that they were some kind of religious sect, but we searched them anyway. They had IDs, apparently issued by the South Vietnamese government, so we let them go.

But later that day we saw them again, this time being loaded onto choppers for a ride to the firebase, probably for inter-rogation. I was glad to see them leave the area, not wholly convinced that they were genuine South Vietnamese civilians.

We camped about a mile south of the firebase that night, and the next morning we were joined by a group of APCs as we headed back to Liz. The tracks, with their .50 caliber machine guns, made me feel very secure. They provided us with the kind of firepower that even the NVA had to respect.

About a half-mile from the hill where Liz was located we jumped on the APCs. As we did I looked back and saw one of the tracks stop to pick up a VC suspect. He looked to be around 15 years old, and as the APC pulled away I saw an old woman running behind and yelling at the driver. The men on the track had tied the young suspect on the front of the vehicle, with ropes running in all directions as though he had been caught in an oversized spider web.

The men on the APC laughed at the old woman as she ran alongside, finally threatening her with their M-16s. She fell behind the column and disappeared as the armored tracks lunged forward and struggled up the muddy road to the top of the hill. I never saw the suspect again.

The next time I made my way back to Duc Pho I met a civilian in a little hootch just down the road from D Company. He represented the Army's college education program, which ironically was based at the University of Wisconsin, the same school that had thrown me out in 1967.

He was an unassuming man of about 45, dressed in civilian clothes and seated behind a wooden table. He was there in Duc Pho for just a few days to serve the men in the brigade who were looking for a course and a few college credits.

I had been out of school for almost two years, and yet I knew that I was going back after I got out of the Army. I had something like 30 credits that would transfer, and I was technically a sophomore. Now I had a chance to test myself against the same standards that I had failed to match 24 months earlier. Finding out how much I had gained, or lost, in two years was an intriguing proposition. I sat down and began to page through the catalog.

"Are you interested in something?"

"Yes, I thing so. I think this English course would be interesting. How does this thing work, anyway?"

"You take these books and do your assignments when you get time. Then you send them into Madison, someone there corrects your lessons, and you get a grade and your papers back in the mail."

"Does it cost anything?"

"Not to members of the Armed Forces."

"That sounds fine, but I'm in the infantry. How can I study in the field?"

"Surely you have a locker or some place where you can keep the books until you get back to camp, don't you?"

"No. Nothing. But I'd like to try it anyway. What do I do?"

"Take these books and sign your name here. You'll need all three of these for Literature 143."

He shoved a pile of books in my direction. They stood about eight inches high and must have weighed five or six pounds.

"This course involves a lot of reading, but I'm sure you'll find it interesting. Here are the assignment sheets, and the envelopes. Send them in as you complete them."

I left the hootch with the books tucked under my left arm. Suddenly I felt different than I had in weeks. I had a new challenge, and new sense of responsibility. I hurried back to the company area and began paging through the books.

I read the first few chapters in Duc Pho, and completed three or four assignments before going back to join D Company in the field. Even out there, when we took a break, I'd take out my new treasures and wallow in the adventures of Natty Bumpo and the practical philosophies of Ben Franklin. They brought me a new sense of fulfillment, a fresh perspective that freed me from the doldrums of the war. They replaced John Wayne and Audie Murphy as my heroes. I became, though quite privately, a kind of storybook snob. I no longer felt the need to seek out other men in the platoon for conversations. I felt akin to Bumpo and Franklin.

As I neared the midpoint of my tour in Vietnam the Brandel conversation began to haunt me more and more. I had been lucky. I had survived for six months as an infantryman. But there was malaria, and ringworm infection, and a few other things that had kept me in the rear much of the time. The next six months could be entirely different. Didn't I owe it to myself to at least try to land a job in the rear? The prospect of a permanent place out of the rain and away from the dangers of the field began to look better and better.

But there was one thing that bothered me. What if I was lucky enough, or skillful enough, to land a job at the PIO, permanently? Wouldn't I feel guilty about the other men in the company who hadn't been as lucky? Was it right for me to use my profile to get a better deal for myself?

I pondered that question for awhile, and came to the conclusion that only an idiot would intentionally remain in the field. Who was I to be so noble? I owed it to myself to get the best deal available. None of the other men would give up a chance to find a spot in the rear, so why should I? Perhaps I had been in the rear too long. Maybe I had forgotten how miserable a night in a mosquito-infested rice paddie could be, or what the field had done to men like Carlson. I'd be a damn fool to pass it up, I told myself. I headed up the road, the first time the company came back to Duc Pho, and located the PIO office. I was anxious to find out whether or not Brandel was telling me the truth about the job opening.

Several men were sitting around the office, casually reading a variety of magazines and newspapers.

"You looking for something?" a voice said. I turned and found a lieutenant sitting to my right.

"Yes sir, I was told you need writers."

"We do," said the officer. He was tall and blond with thinning hair and a friendly smile. "See Lieutenant Cobb over there."

He pointed to a desk at the far end of the hootch. Seated there was another lieutenant, busily looking over some papers. His hair was dark and cut very short, and he looked very businesslike.

"Sir," I said, "my name is PFC Reich. I understand you need writers."

"We sure do," he said, popping out of his chair to grab my hand. "You a writer?"

"No sir... well, I think I can write. I had a few English courses in college and..."

"Good. Come back here this evening about five and we'll give you a little test. Okay?"

"Yes sir, I'll be here at five. Thanks."

The fact that there was an opening was encouraging. But I still belonged to D Company, and it wasn't likely that they were going to let me go without a permanent profile. In spite of that I went back to the PIO hootch at 5:00 P.M. and found Lieutenant Cobb waiting for me.

"Take this paper and sit down here, in front of the radio. In a few minutes an AFVN newscast will come on. I want you to get as many little stories out of that newscast as you can. Take your notes, then write two or three sentences per story. This is how I want it to look."

He handed me a sheet of paper with several stories that had been summarized from the newscast on the previous day.

"We pass this out each morning to the officers in the mess hall. They like to keep up on what's going on. The man who does it for us now will rotate in a couple of weeks, and it's hard to find a good writer who can do the job. You'd better get ready... the newscast will be on in a couple of minutes."

He walked quickly back to his desk and began shuffling through some papers.

I had never done anything like it before. This was clearly no English paper that I could do at my leisure. It demanded some skills that I wasn't sure I had.

But I listened and wrote quickly. I missed two or three stories completely, but I had notes on a dozen more. I sat down at the typewriter and began to compose my paragraphs. After about fifteen minutes I told Lieutenant Cobb that I had finished. He rose quickly and walked rapidly to my typewriter. He stood over me for several minutes, reading each story and showing no emotion. I was sure he was looking through the paper, trying to find a decent way to let me down. I felt I had done nothing but waste his time and embarrass myself.

But it wasn't that way. He looked up, smiled broadly, and extended his hand.

"Welcome to the PIO," he said, shaking my hand vigorously.

I couldn't believe my ears. I tried not to show my excitement.

"Thank you, sir," I said. "What happens next?"

"Well, I'll send a note down to your company asking them to release you. I'm sure they will. It's just a matter of paper work. Why don't you come back in the morning and begin work. You can do that, can't you?"

"I think so, sir. I still have a few days left on my profile."

I went back to the company area, elated over my apparent success at getting a position in the PIO. It was incredible, I thought. Was it really the end of my field duty? Was I going to give up my rucksack for good, getting a permanent bunk and a footlocker, and three hot meals a day? Could I have seen the last of my days in the field and those cold, depressing nights?

I told myself it was too good to be true. Somehow, things just weren't going to work out. D Company was too short on man-power to grant my release without a fight. I had been away from the company for so long that I didn't even know the company commander's name. Why should he do me any favors?

The PIO needed a writer, but D Company needed warm bodies in the field a lot worse. I had the feeling that the RAMFs were going to do their best to stop the transfer, from the clerks on up to the first sergeant. After all, they had a stake in the game, too. The more men they could keep in the field, the less likely it was that they would ever have to go themselves. And it had happened before. Some companies became so desperate that they called out their supply men and their clerks to keep the ranks from becoming too thin. There was no reason to believe it couldn't happen in D Company, and they knew it. That's why they did their best to keep the profiles down. It was the "better you than me" philosophy, and I was sure it would spell the end of my dream to escape to the PIO.

I worked for a few days in the PIO office, taking assignments from a specialist 4 who served as the editor of the brigade news-paper. My first assignment was to rewrite a description of a firebase that had the byline "L. Fedorski." It was supposed to be a feature story, but even I knew that it didn't have much hope. It was just too dull. I worked on it for two hours. It ended up in the wastebasket.

Later I saw Fedorski, who was actually a photographer, and of all things, a cartoonist. He had a private cubicle in the back of the PIO office where he worked by himself on his cartoon strip. It was weeks before we talked again.

I conducted at least one interview during that first few days. I was assigned the job of gathering information on the heroic actions of a captain who worked in the brigade commander's office. The man I had to interview was a lieutenant colonel, and it was only his experience and sensitivity that kept me from blowing the whole thing. In short, he conducted the interview and told me what to write. He lauded the captain for jumping out of helicopter and slaying four or five Vietcong suspects. He killed them by lobbing grenades into their bunker.

I wrote the story and turned it in, and a few days later my profile ended. I asked the lieutenant what could be done, but he said my release hadn't come through yet.

"Just go back for awhile and we'll work it out," he told me.

I should have used the puffiness in my legs to get an extension on my profile, but I didn't. I guess I was sick and tired of running from one doctor to another without getting any permanent results. Instead I packed my gear and joined the platoon on a firebase a few miles from Duc Pho. It wasn't long before the grapevine was buzzing about some kind of "major mission." I was sure I had seen the last of the PIO.

The company flew off Liz one morning in what turned out to be a pretty large combat assault. There must have been 20 choppers loaded with troops. We flew west, maybe ten miles from the coast, until we were floating over a valley surrounded by two large, greenish-blue hills, covered from head to toe with thick vegetation. We could see that we were opening up a completely new area; there was no sign of a friendly firebase anywhere.

The choppers dropped to the floor of the valley as gunshots circled around us, pouring rockets and mini-gun fire into the hillsides. The noise added to the urgency of the situation.

Fortunately, there was no enemy resistance; I had been lucky once again. We dropped into the valley and left our choppers. Each platoon set up its own perimeter. After a few minutes we formed a file and began walking up the valley.

That night we camped under a bright moon. The grass in the rice paddies was long and moist, and I fell asleep to the annoying hum of mosquitoes outside my poncho, which I had wound around me like a cocoon. The mosquito repellent didn't seem to help. I poured as much onto my neck and face as I could stand, and even soaked my shirt with it. I felt like a greased pig, and probably smelled like one, too.

The next day we moved along a river to a place where the water was trickling out of the mountains. It was a wide, but gentle stream that slowly crawled over huge rocks as it made its way to the valley below. We headed up the river single file. It seemed like we walked for an hour before we rested. The rocks were large and very slippery, and it was rough going. The only casualty, however, was a skinny German Shepherd that had come along to help uncover enemy base-camps. He had cut his leg trying to jump from one rock to another, and a medevac chopper was called in to take him back to the rear for medical attention. The lucky GI who served as his trainer went along.

About a quarter of a mile up the stream we turned to the west and began climbing up a steep slope. In a minute or two we were standing next to a row of impressive holes in the ground, and they were obviously fresh. The ground was rocky, and large boulders rested at the bottom of the pits. It was the first time I had seen the work of a B-52 raid close up. It was very impressive. Apparently intelligence had spotted an enemy base camp there, and we were there to mop-up the operation.

There was little immediate sign of the enemy's presence, except for some blood that had been splattered on the nearby trees. Later that evening a second, irritating sign appeared. Thousands of pesky gnats, drawn by the smell of death, haunted us during the 48 hours we rested along the banks of the stream.

We set up for the night, and as usual, each man had to devise his own shelter. There was nothing but the bare ground, a few spindly trees, and our ponchos to work with. I couldn't find the energy or the imagination to build my own hootch, so I sat on a rock near my rucksack, smoking a cigarette and praying that it wouldn't rain. I was lucky. Only a few sprinkles came that night.

Early the next morning, we began a search of the area surrounding the camp. Our platoon was ordered to look further up the hill and almost directly behind the camp. We really had no idea how long before the NVA had evacuated the camp. Maybe they were waiting in ambush up ahead, or maybe they had seen the impressive combat assault and raced for the shelter of the jungles near Laos. We didn't know where they were, or how many there were. All we knew was that they had left no weapons or bodies behind for us to find.

We soon discovered that the other platoons were also searching the area above the camp. The whole thing reminded me of an Easter egg hunt. We were like children racing to find the biggest prize. The hunt really got a boost when the word filtered down that a group of free-lancing GIs had wandered even further west and uncovered a cache of around 15 NVA weapons. Now souvenirs were involved, and we went about our work with renewed enthusiasm.

But nothing more was found that day, and we drifted back to the campsite. When we returned we found a group of D Company men, not from the 2nd platoon, digging under a huge rock. Apparently someone had spotted some freshly-dug earth near the base of the huge boulder. In a minute they uncovered a hand, and then an arm, and finally a body. It was the remains of an NVA soldier, and he was dragged out into the open for a closer inspection.

He was a young soldier, with his eyes open and his body twisted grotesquely. He was wearing a green uniform, and he was the first NVA I had ever seen up close. Soon a second body was uncovered, and he was also pulled out of the shallow grave. Neither man had any obvious wounds, but dried blood that had trickled from their ears told us they had been killed by the concussion of the B-52 attack.

I stood and observed the two bodies for several minutes. Several other GIs did, too. The sudden appearance of the two NVA regulars almost made up for the disappointment we felt for not finding any weapons up the hill, and most of the men were soon laughing and joking as they stood over the corpses.

One of the men, a big machine gunner by the name of Jones, noticed that one of the dead men had a large gold tooth in the back of his mouth. Without hesitating he took out a hunting knife and extracted the tooth, carefully placing it in his shirt pocket. Then he noticed that the same man was wearing a gold ring. He yanked at the ring for several minutes, but the swollen flesh refused to surrender. Finally, he took the knife and cut off the finger. When he did I turned away.

Later a search of the bodies turned up two wallets with North Vietnamese currency in them. The bills were passed around, and like every other man in the platoon, I took one and put it in my own wallet. But I took it out a half hour later and gave it to someone else. I guess it was simple superstition. I didn't want any part of Vietnam to follow me home, particularly something that came from a dead enemy soldier.

The two North Vietnamese soldiers were finally returned to their grave and covered over with rocks and dirt. The two body counts were phoned into headquarters a few minutes later.

One of the most fascinating things about the camp was the massive terrace of trees that formed the slope on the opposite side of the water. It was so thick that it seemed a man could walk over the top without touching the ground. It was acres and acres of dense jungle, the kind that could hide a battalion of enemy soldiers or a field hospital.

I kept watching it for some sign of movement. I was sure someone was watching us as we sat on our side of the river just 200 yards away. I knew that if an NVA machine gun zeroed in on us, there would be no place to hide. I felt like a sitting duck.

But the vast jungle greenery proved innocent, never erupting as I had imagined it might.

We left the camp a day later, quietly and unceremoniously, in single file. In an hour we were once again sitting in the deep grasses of the valley below, watching a glowing orange Vietnam sunset and waiting for a hot meal to come on a re-supply chopper.

Later, as we ate, I overheard some of the men talking about the possibility that D Company was scheduled for a place called "Pinkville." They also called it My Lai, and said it was notorious for booby traps. D Company had been there a few months earlier, according to one of the men, and it was chewed up pretty badly. His voice, as much as his words, told me that I didn't even want to see the place.

Some of the men plotted openly to get themselves out of the field. I plotted silently, but with equal enthusiasm.

We spent a quiet night in the valley, and in the morning we sat around for several hours in the hot sun before we received our orders to move out.

As we packed, a new lieutenant walked by, a man I had never seen before. To my surprise, he was temporarily in command of the entire company. At that instant I had an idea. I walked over to him and asked if he would take a minute to look at my leg.

"I'd like you to see this, sir," I said, trying to sound worried.

He was a baby-faced kid with a spanking new haircut and a uniform that still had its rich, dark green color. He looked to be around 20, perhaps a year or two older.

He followed me to a large rock where I untied my shoe and rolled up my pants, exposing my water-filled leg. Then I pressed my finger into the swollen flesh, nearly pushing to the bone. It left a deep impression, and as usual, the hole remained for several seconds.

The young lieutenant's eyes almost came out of his head, and his mouth dropped open.

"Can you walk?" he asked, looking like a little boy who had just seen his first garden snake.

"Yes sir," I said, mustering as much sincerity as I could.

"We've got a chopper coming in with chow tonight, maybe a half mile up the trail. You be on it."

"Yes sir, I will."

He stood up and walked away. Instead of scoffing at my leg, he had shown some genuine concern. I was sure he would ask to see a profile, or some other evidence to prove that I was really ill. But he didn't. I had gambled on a longshot, and I had won. Of course my trip to the rear would be short-lived, but that didn't matter. At least I might be able to buy a few more days in Duc Pho while the company moved north to Pinkville. That could be enough to save me. And besides, he had ordered me to go back. That was something that the first sergeant, or the other RAMFs, couldn't argue with.

I felt a little guilty about putting one over on the new officer, but not guilty enough to turn back. The situation was desperate. I was no longer ashamed to take advantage of my disability.

Our walk up the trail to the landing zone was uneventful, but with every step my fear grew. I kept thinking, if I can just make it to that chopper, everything is going to work out.

A re-supply chopper could be heard in the distance as we set up a perimeter at the far end of the valley. It settled down gently, and wound to a stop as hot food and a bag of mail were being unloaded.

Among my letters was an envelope from the USAFI group in Madison. I had sent in four lessons, and this was the first one to come back. I opened it and found, to my surprise, that I had scored a 92 on the first lesson. Only 24 months earlier I wouldn't have thought that I could ever achieve such lofty heights.

The chopper finally cranked up, and I scrambled aboard. I didn't even look back at my platoon. I was a bit ashamed to be deserting them again, but my safety counted more than their opinions, perhaps for the first time since I had come to Vietnam. Now I was like Carlson, scheming constantly to get myself out of the field. I decided that the edema in my leg was the best thing that had ever happened to me. Even if my legs would have to be taken off later on, I was better off with the infection than without. No legs was still preferable to death.

As the chopper circled to gain altitude, it was the target of several sniper rounds. It seemed a fitting way for me to make my exit from the field. Fortunately, none of them hit their target.

My good fortune continued when I got to the rear. The PIO still wanted me, and my company was only lukewarm to the idea of forcing me back into the field. They were probably surprised to see that Lieutenant Cobb showed so much interest in me. Maybe they figured that if I couldn't make it as a grunt, the PIO was the best place to ship me. Maybe they just thought that I was more trouble than I was worth.

I worked in the PIO office for several days, doing little projects like the evening news sheet and biding my time while I waited for yet another examination.

Then one morning the company called and said my time for R & R had arrived. I was scheduled to leave for Tokyo in two days. I raced down to D Company and began to make preparations for the trip. As I completed my business with the company clerk, the first sergeant walked in and stood next to me. He had a half-grin on his face. He said the new company commander, Captain Blackman, was ordering everybody to the field who didn't have a permanent profile. That, of course, applied to me, but R & R would come first.

"When you get back," the first sergeant said, "you might be doing this."

He marched in place, his shoulders curled to simulate the weight of a rucksack. He smiled broadly, knowing how much discomfort he had created in me. But I didn't say a word. I didn't want to do anything that might jeopardize my nine days in Tokyo. I finished my business and left.

೮ಽ

I thought it might be hard to get used to civilian clothes again, but it wasn't. In fact, it felt good. I almost felt like I had been lifted out of the Army, permanently, although I knew better. I had nine days ahead of me on R & R, and no more. The second half of my tour, clouded by uncertainty, was just around the corner.

But as I sat on the plane, cruising toward another country, I pondered the possibility of not going back. It was nothing more than a flirtation, but I dreamed of skipping out on my return flight and catching a plane for the states. Tokyo would give me that chance. I saw the carrot dangling at the end of the string.

But becoming a deserter just wasn't in me. Even though I had learned how men could die in Vietnam, and in fact were dying, I still wasn't convinced that the same thing was going to happen to me. I knew, deep down, that I might be blown to bits by a landmine, or have my head split in two by a sniper's bullet, but I couldn't just run back home. I was afraid all right, but not crazy with fear. I kept telling myself, convinced that I was only being coldly logical, that it was better to die than to live with the shame of having run away from the war. Not going back to Vietnam was tempting, but it wasn't much of an option. I had to spend my twelve months in Vietnam, or die trying.

It was my sixth month overseas, and I no longer dreamed of medals and John Wayne heroics. Nor did I stick with Vietnam because I loved my country, or hated communism. I was going back in nine days out of fear. The perils of combat haunted me, and thought that I might die before my 22nd birthday tied my stomach in a knot, but I knew I couldn't bear to think of the avalanche of shame that would shadow my family if I ran away.

I wondered about people back home who had committed suicide. Supposedly they feared living more than death. It never made any sense to me, until I got to Vietnam. Going to war, after all, was a close cousin to suicide. It was a gamble, less certain than putting a gun to my head, but capable of providing the same consequences. Vietnam was Russian roulette on a grand scale. The chamber would rotate every day, for 365 days, and if I was lucky, it would always be empty. I was simply willing to take that chance. Even a live round was better than going home a deserter. Death was clearly the lesser of two evils.

I took a single room in a place called the "Western Hotel." It was a modern, six-story structure, somewhere in downtown Tokyo. I bought a good Japanese radio in a nearby shop, and later a cheap, Polaroid camera to take back to Vietnam. I also bought a coin set and sent it home to my brother, Jon, for his collection. The rest of my money, something in the neighborhood of $200, went for food and liquor.

I sat every night in the hotel bar, drinking one Tom Collins after another, and watching Japanese television. Sometimes I chatted with other GIs when they came around, but it was usually just the bartender and me. That suited me fine. I wanted to be alone and to forget who and where I was, and the drinks helped. The hours crept by at times, but I didn't mind. It seemed to push Vietnam further and further into the background.

Occasionally a prostitute or two would wander into the bar, and sometimes they wanted to know if I was interested in buying them for the night for $65. I always said no. Some of them tried to shame me into spending the night with them by hinting that I might be homosexual, but it didn't matter. I couldn't have cared less what they thought.

I spent one afternoon reading an English newspaper and listening to the radio up in my room. The American station carried a football game between teams of American GI all-stars. It amazed me that as the casualty list in Vietnam was growing longer and longer, other young American GIs, drafted into the same Army, were squaring off on a sunny afternoon to play football. I felt like we were all a million miles from the war.

A hundred-thousand men were up to their knees in the field in Vietnam at the moment, while a few lucky GIs were passing their tour playing a football game. It didn't seem right at all. It just wasn't fair. But "fair" was a word that no longer applied. The world, I was slowly learning, was really divided into two groups: the lucky and the unlucky. It was really quite simple. The men in Japan were lucky. The men in Vietnam were not. It made no sense to try and understand it. That's just the way it was.

Equally insane was the fact that I was sitting in a hotel room, surrounded by pimps and prostitutes, all working desperately to relieve me of my money. As long as the war continued, and the GIs kept coming, life was good for them. The war was an opportunity that they couldn't pass up. What did they care about the domino theory or the politics of Vietnam?

There was one evening, toward the end of my stay in Tokyo, which was very different from the others. Rather, it was a woman who made the difference. She was a young prostitute, lavishly dressed and quite beautiful, who had wandered into the bar around ten one night and sat just a couple of stools away. She seemed a class above the others, a professional's professional. We began to talk, and she offered to spend the night in my room. The price, again, was $65. I declined, though I nearly had enough drinks that night to give in. Maybe I was afraid of something. I wasn't sure. But I had told her no, and she finally left.

I had never bought the idea that only a crazy man would die a virgin in Vietnam, unless he had no other choice. A lot of men believed that, though. It was a kind of superstition, but it never made much of an impression on me. Besides, I wasn't going to die, and if I did, my experience in bed wouldn't make much difference.

I tried to read the paper when I got back to my room that night, but I was too drunk. I fell asleep listening to the radio.

Two days later I flew back to Chu Lai and later Duc Pho. I prayed that my orders for the PIO had finally come through, but I still had that feeling, deep down, that I might be back in the field within the next 24 hours.

Chapter 7
A Dream Comes True

It was almost a relief to get back to Duc Pho. I was never very fond of traveling. And somehow the apprehension I should have experienced just wasn't there. I guess I had accepted the idea that I was about to be dragged back to the field, and there was nothing anyone could do about it. I naturally hoped for a chance to remain in the rear, but I was prepared for the worst.

I reported back to the PIO after checking in with my company. I still had temporary status with Lieutenant Cobb's outfit, so I thought I'd make D Company chase me when it was ready to send me out. Maybe they'd forget about me for a few days, maybe longer.

I was introduced that first morning to the new brigade editor, Carl Nord. Lieutenant Peleate asked him to show me to the writer's hootch, one of two occupied by the PIO. The other belonged to the photographers.

Nord was a specialist 4, one rank above me, but I knew from the beginning that he wasn't going to pay much attention to the chain of command. He contrasted sharply with the tall dark-haired, sober-faced editor I had seen in the office a month earlier. Nord was less than six feet tall and very thin, and his hair dropped to the center of his forehead. With a sprinkling of freckles and an exaggerated grin, he looked a lot like an adult version of Dennis the Menace. He poured out a steady stream of one-liners, poking fun at the Army whenever he got the chance. After each joke he'd tilt his head, flash a smile, and squint until his eyes were nearly closed. I didn't quite know what to make of him. I was still too nervous about my status to offend anyone, so I smiled back, thinking all the time that Carl Nord was one of the most peculiar people I had ever met.

Nord showed me to the back of the hootch. It was a typical, six-man tent with a plywood floor and three sagging mattresses along each side of the aisle. Each bed had a dark green mosquito net, draped over a thin metal frame. There was a standup metal locker at the foot of each bed, and a footlocker on a nearby table.

The tent was dark and gloomy, probably because the screened openings at either end of the hootch were covered with dust, apparently from the low-flying helicopters that took off and landed nearby.

I put away my gear and returned to the PIO office, which was about 200 yards to the east of the two hootches. There I found a place to sit, hoping for a chance to write a story that would demonstrate my value to the office, I felt like the whole PIO experience was a dead end, a very temporary situation. I expected a phone call at any minute from D Company, telling me to pack my gear and get back to the field.

Surprisingly, the call didn't come for the first two weeks. Then, one afternoon, Lieutenant Cobb delivered the bad news. My old company, with its new gung-ho commander, was calling all able-bodied men back for a quick flight to the field. The captain had suspended all temporary leaves for people like myself. Lieutenant Cobb said that even profiles were being shipped out, a real change from the old policy.

"What can I do?" said Cobb, shrugging. "He's a captain. I'm only a lieutenant."

He told me I could stay the night, but the following day I would have to head back.

As much as I had tried to prepare myself for that moment, it still fell on me like a 500-pound rock. I was too upset at the news to say anything. Cobb turned and walked quickly back to his desk.

He knew what it meant for someone to be going back to the field after experiencing a stay in the rear. I was sure he wanted me to stay, since he needed new writers, but the chain of command couldn't be overlooked. I had no chance to appeal, no opportunity to reverse the order. I was just glad that I had been given one extra night out of the rain.

The following day brought more unexpected news. Cobb had apparently sent an appeal to some major in Duc Pho, and he, in turn, phoned the D Company commander and ordered him to cut my release orders. It meant that I was being granted a permanent transfer to the PIO.

I could hardly believe it. It was the greatest gift that I had ever received. It was like ten Christmases rolled into one. It was almost a guarantee that I would make it home in June when my tour ended. The misery, and possible death in the field, were suddenly behind me. I felt as though everything was turning around for me, and obviously it was. The PIO not only provided me with greater safety, it gave me a future as well. My status in D Company was almost nil. I was a dirty grunt, a private first class with little prospect for advancement in rank or responsibility.

But the PIO had changed all that. I was trading my M-16 for a notepad and a pencil, moving from the mud of the field to the relative cleanliness of an office in Duc Pho. There would be clean clothes every day, polished boots, hot meals, movies, and best of all, respect. I had sudden status as a reporter. In the field no one would bother to tell me what was going on. Now officers would seek me out to get their names in the brigade newspaper. I had, by some stroke of luck, been dealt a hand filled with trump cards. My days in the field made me appreciate it, and I was determined to do everything in my power to keep as much distance as possible between me and my old life on the line.

සෝ

Although Duc Pho was somewhat of a forward firebase, it gave me an immense sense of security. Our hootch was more than 200 yards from the perimeter, a long way for a sapper to travel once he broke through the wire. We could always be hit by mortar rounds, of course, but from what I had heard, those kinds of attacks were rare. Occasionally a round or two would be aimed at the choppers on the pad, or the radar installation, but that was it.

There was one other advantage. Duc Pho had more than its share of firepower. It had ample .50 caliber machine guns, and even a battery or two of artillery pieces. The chances that we would be the object of a full-fledged ground assault were slim, I thought. It would take another Tet for that to happen, and a second offensive like that wasn't likely, not after the NVA had suffered such incredible losses in January 1968.

Just being on the inside of the perimeter was security enough. I no longer had to carry a weapon wherever I went. I kept my M-16 in my locker, hoping that it could stay there until my tour ended six months later.

Life in the rear soon settled into a kind of comfortable routine. Nord assigned me the task of putting out the daily newsletter for the mess hall, and I also did an occasional story. Nord was an experienced writer with a degree from Drake University. He knew my limitations, and he was a patient teacher. He was just trying to put in his time, but he took his job seriously. He wanted to put out the best possible newspaper, and for that I respected him. The longer I knew him, the more I liked him.

Like me, Nord had been rescued from the ranks of the infantry. His salvation, however, had come at almost the same minute he landed in Vietnam. Apparently he spent a week or two in the field, though, because he told one story about an incident several months earlier.

He said he was on a mission one day when his unit came upon a suspected enemy hootch. They found a middle-aged man inside, and Nord was assigned to guard him while the rest of the men searched the nearby area. Nord said he sat with a .45 pistol in his lap, watching the man, who was smiling and chattering in Vietnamese. Then, when Nord looked away for a second, the man lunged forward. Nord raised the gun instinctively and fired point blank. The round hit the suspect in the head, and he fell to the ground. He died a few minutes later after gasping for air. When Nord came to the end of the story he made a sucking sound, illustrating the man's death rattle.

During my first week with the PIO, Nord suggested that we order patches for our right shoulders. He wanted them to read "combat correspondent." He asked me what I thought, and I said "why not?" Lieutenant Cobb approved of the idea, and a week later the patches were delivered from the Korean tailors just around the corner.

The patches seemed to me to be rather juvenile at first, but when I found out how impressed a lot of people were when they read "combat correspondent," I changed my mind.

ơ

Each morning I got up around 7:30 and went to the office an hour later. By then the sun was already quite hot. Every day was pretty much the same. We didn't pay much attention to the calendar, seldom distinguishing one day of the week from another. They were just numbers, really, and the only number that mattered to each man was the time that remained on his tour.

We recognized holidays, of course, like Christmas and New Year's, mostly because cease-fires were in effect during those periods. But even during those "time outs" there was violence and death. Cease-fires were actually uncomfortable times, because we still couldn't relax. Violations were numerous on both sides. Still, the lull gave us renewed hope just as the peace talks had done in 1968 when they first began in Paris.

During that same year the United States elected a new president. I sat in the PIO bunker between our hootch and the photographers' hootch, making out my absentee ballot on the day of the election. I voted for Richard Nixon, hoping that he would speed up the war's end. I even told Nord, obviously kidding, that he should pack his bags, because Nixon was going to pull us soon. He laughed. No one really believed the war was about to end. The final days were nowhere in sight. But it didn't matter. This war wasn't like the others. This time, there was no serving in the Army "for the duration."

When I joined the PIO I knew I would have to show up each morning in fairly clean fatigues, and that concerned me. Would I have to wash my own clothes, iron them, and polish my boots every night?

Fortunately, none of that was necessary. There was a woman from the village named Mamasan Lin who took care of all our domestic needs. She served both hootches, collecting a dollar a day from each one. She was around 25, thin and fair. Her hair was long and black, and she wore it in a ponytail. She was sky, like most Vietnamese, but we soon learned that she was intelligent and had a good sense of humor. When she smiled, she displayed a bright silver tooth in the front of her mouth. We called her "mamasan" for short, and we soon became very fond of her.

Mamasan washed our clothes by stomping them with her bare feet in a small plastic bowl filled with water and detergent. Later she would iron them and polish our boots, and naturally she swept the floor each day. She seemed to be comfortable in the compound, and we didn't know if she had a family until she showed up at the gate one morning with two little children.

The boy was around five, and his sister was slightly younger. They had black hair and large, brown eyes. They stayed close to their mother, never uttering a word. They impressed me, because they were so tiny and innocent. They made me think about the sapper attacks that came all to frequently in the village, where the VC would indiscriminately throw satchel charges into civilian hootches as a part of their terrorist tactics, killing innocent women and children. It seemed like such an immoral way to fight a war. It hurt me to think that they were living in an unprotected area, scrambling from their beds at night to a dirt bunker when the mortars fell. They were beautiful, innocent little kids, unable to understand the violence that surrounded them. It hurt me to look at their faces.

Every night the company bar would open around five and serve ice cold soda and beer. The bar was directly in front of our hootch, no more than 50 feet away. It was wonderfully convenient.

Our hootch had its own lawn chairs, a table, and even a guitar. Electricity was another luxury, although we had a problem keeping light bulbs. The hootch had one on each end, but they were constantly being stolen while we were away at the PIO hootch. When the supply tent ran out we lowered ourselves to scrounging them from other living quarters in the company area. We always went around during the supper hour, looking for an abandoned hootch with a light bulb near the doorway. The round robin theft got so bad that we finally settled for a single bulb, as did most of the other hootches.

One of my most valuable possessions was a small, round plastic washbowl. It was dark green, about twelve inches in diameter, and it rested on a shelf just above my bed. I don't know why it was never stolen, but I kept it until I left Vietnam. Each morning I would fill it with water and brush my teeth, wash my face, and then shave, in that order. That kept me from having to go after a refill. I was always careful to brush my teeth first, sucking water from the middle of the bowl to rinse my mouth when I was finished. I never trusted the bowl enough to drink from the edge, probably because nearly every morning I had to empty mice droppings from it before I filled it with water.

One night I found a mousetrap and baited it with a peanut wrapped in a piece of tape, the way my father had once shown me. After I shut out the light and went to bed, it took less than a minute before the trap was sprung on the shelf just over-head. I threw the little victim outside, reset the trap, and turned out the light again. In a matter of seconds the trap was sprung for a second time. Again I threw the dead mouse outdoors, and set the trap for the third time. In the morning I found the peanut was gone. I never bothered to try and catch another mouse while I was in Duc Pho. It was a hopeless cause; there were just too many of them.

The mess hall was just 30 seconds north of the PIO hootches. We each had metal trays which we kept in our area, and after each meal we'd submerge them in boiling water to keep them clean. But the low-flying helicopters kept them covered with a thin layer of dust as they hung near our bunks. It was something we learned to live with.

The food that was served in the Duc Pho mess hall never impressed me. I didn't care much for roast beef, but it seemed as though every other meal was built around roast beef. One day, during lunch, it was actually offered as a side dish, decorated with lettuce. I walked through the line that day without even dirtying my tray, and opened a can of pork and beans back at the hootch.

One day, while I was in Chu Lai some weeks later, I stood in line with some Marines, waiting for a dinner as I passed through. I overheard the men in front of me complaining that the meal was chicken—again. I remember thinking that chicken hadn't gotten as far south as Duc Pho in weeks. I figured it was a matter of being in the right place along the re-supply line. It was like the men in the rear who re-supplied the men in the field. Somebody always had first choice.

℣

Duc Pho, to my surprise, had its own PX. It wasn't much of a building, though, just a tiny hootch, maybe 20 by 40, made of plywood with a tin roof. It was closed as much as it was open, mostly because it ran out of things to sell hours after the word got out that it had been re-supplied. When it did open men would wait in line for an hour or more, since no more than six men were allowed inside at one time. The items for sale were on shelves that stood against the walls. The GIs walked around, moving from one shelf to another, looking carefully before they bought. There was always one man on duty, and no cash register. It was a pretty simple operation, compared to the spacious PX in Chu Lai with its tiled floors and glass cases filled with expensive radios and cameras.

The sparseness of the shelves in the PX, sometimes bearing no more than five or six items, made for an interesting study in human behavior. American GIs, who had grown up with stores brimming with thousands of brightly colored packages, suddenly found themselves in a most unusual setting. If a man was in a hurry he could shop and be out of the PX in a matter of minutes. Most of the time the whole stock consisted of shoe polish, nuts, corn curls in metal containers, handkerchiefs, and beans. There was no such thing as a choice between two similar items.

Yet it always amazed me that men would stand for several minutes in front of the shelves, acting as though they were scouting for just the right brand. I wondered who they were trying to kid. I finally concluded that they were either day-dreaming about home, or they had a lot of time to waste.

It also amazed me that the GIs waiting outside never protested to their poky buddies. The PX, I guess, was more of a museum than a store, with the items on the shelf representing a happy memory from the world we had left behind. I guess they figured that each man had the right to spend as much time as he wanted in the little hootch. After all, unless the shelves ran dry, they would soon be enjoying the same casual browsing.

By reading every newspaper and magazine that came into the office I developed a fairly reliable newswriting style. The practice of doing the daily reports for the officers' mess also helped. I would listen to the newscast over AFVN around 5:00 P.M., and then carve out eight to twelve paragraphs on news about the war and life back in the States.

Nord had the duty of putting out the nightly report on the brigade's activities. He'd check with brigade headquarters around 6:00 P.M. taking his information from a large map covered with a sheet of clear plastic that hung in a prominent place in a bunker that was in the center of the camp. On the sheet were marked the day's kills, weapons captured, VC suspects taken in the field, and other pertinent, statistical information. After Nord put his information together at the typewriter, he would call it up to Americal headquarters in Chu Lai.

The brigade headquarters, that large, reinforced bunker where the daily activity map was located, served as the nerve center for the entire 11th Brigade. There were telephones and radios everywhere. It impressed me because it seemed so well-built, apparently capable of taking any round in the enemy's arsenal. It was the one place in camp where I felt completely safe.

Later I inherited Nord's evening duties, which was a step up from the mess hall newsletter. I got to the point where I could crank out the daily report in something like 15 minutes at the typewriter. That left more time for other things, like sweeping the PIO office, which was another of my duties, or catching the nightly movie.

While I was involved in some rather routine chores, I also worked on features about the brigade. To do that, I usually had to travel by helicopter to a forward firebase.

Once, however, a story walked into the office that turned out to be a lot more than I first imagined. A dog handler by the name of Carstens wandered by one day to visit with another man in the office. While he was drinking a Coke, I picked up a clipboard and began to make a few notes. He talked about his dog and his training, and how his canine partner had saved his life one afternoon by keeping him from walking into a booby-trapped area along the trail.

Weeks later, while I was paging through the _Army Reporter_, I found the story on Carstens. It was the first time that any of my work had made it beyond Chu Lai. I cut it out and put it up on the bulletin board for everyone in the office to see. It was my only real accomplishment up to that point, and it greatly boosted my self-confidence as a self-made journalist.

While my writing was on the upswing, my "news sense" was still very primitive. The fact was pointed out to me in February when Tony, another brigade writer, returned from LZ Cork with a story that he assured us would be "big time." He had interviewed a sergeant who was on Cork when it was overrun a couple of nights earlier. The sergeant was dragged halfway down the side of the hill by two Vietcong who were bent on making him a POW. He escaped, but only after pulverizing his two would-be captors with a steady barrage of punches.

Tony, a Texan, was outspoken and self-confident. I liked him, but I recognized that blowing things out of proportion was one of his faults. That's why I didn't pay much attention to him when he came back from Cork.

Before he sat down to write his story, he paced nervously in the office, puffing on a cigarette and recounting the interview in great detail. I thought he was wasting his time, and so did most of the other men in the office. A story without guns and bullets seldom made it, even Chu Lai. How did he expect to peddle a piece that involved nothing more than a wrestling match between a GI and two sappers?

Tony took the whole next day to finish his story. He sat in the corner, puffing away on cigarettes and laboring in silence. I couldn't help but laugh at his apparent foolishness.

A week later, however, Tony burst into the office with the latest copy of _Stars and Stripes_. We opened it to page five and found his article spread across the top of the page, printed word for word. We shrunk with embarrassment. Tony's story made him the front-runner in the office, and gave the rest of us a goal to shoot for.

CR

On Christmas day, 1968, I jumped on a helicopter with a photographer and followed a couple of chaplains out to a forward firebase where they were going to conduct a short service. There we met a captain, obviously the company commander. He was a large man, put together in the mold of a football lineman, and very casual. He invited us to make ourselves at home while he got the men together for the service.

While the photographer took pictures, I wandered over to a foxhole where a group of GIs were relaxing. I still hadn't done much interviewing, but I was sure a story about men serving in Vietnam on Christmas day wouldn't be too difficult to gather, or write.

I identified myself and began what I thought would be the perfect question.

"How does it feel to be in Vietnam on Christmas?" I asked, standing ready with my pencil and pen.

The GI looked away for a minute.

"Shitty," he said.

I didn't know how to react. I shook my head in agreement, and looked at the next man.

"How about you. How do you like being in Vietnam on Christmas?"

"It's like he said, shitty."

I smiled with embarrassment, trying to find a way to leave gracefully. I put my pencil away and folded up my pad.

"Well," I said quietly, "thanks for the interview." I turned and walked away.

We spent about an hour on the firebase. After the service was over, the captain approached the chaplains and asked if one of them would mind saying a few words for some men who had been killed the day before. The Catholic chaplain, a major, followed the company commander to a spot where four helmets sat in a neat row on the ground. Some of the other grunts gathered around them. They all bowed their heads while the chaplain said a prayer. A few of the men were misty-eyed when he finished.

Later I asked someone what had happened. He said the company had been humping along through some thick jungle when it suddenly came upon an NVA base camp. The NVA opened fire first, killing the four men who were walking at the head of the patrol.

The short memorial service had a sobering effect on all of us. No one said a word as the helicopter made its way back to Duc Pho.

∞

Somehow Lou Fedorski (Fedo) and I ended up working together for most of the months I spent with the PIO. It was a pretty good combination. I wrote, and he took the pictures. And we both liked the idea of getting away from the office for a few days. Fedo was particularly unhappy about having two officers, Cobb and Peleate, looking in on him from time to time. When the chance came to spend a few days traveling, he didn't hesitate to go.

Fedo, the office cartoonist, was the only man with a private working area, and he liked it that way. He had enlisted for three years, but he was sorely disillusioned with the Army and Vietnam. He hated any mention of spit and polish, and particularly, inspections. He didn't like to salute officers. Anything that seemed to distinguish military life from civilian life got under his skin. All he wanted, he told me, was to do his cartoon strip and be left alone.

Fedo was just 21, like me, but he had already been married for a year. He often missed his wife, and sometimes in the evening he'd go off by himself and sit for hours, reading letters from home. He seemed lonelier than most of the other men, and the war around him didn't help. He felt the frustrations of being caught in the middle of Vietnam, like the rest of us, but he seemed to feel it deeper.

Fedo was sensitive, and that might have been the reason why we got along so well. Whatever the reason, we hung together for months, and when I got an assignment, there was no question that Fedo would serve as my photographer.

Our first assignment involved, of all things, a computer that helped the artillery units find their targets. It was located on a base two miles west of Duc Pho. We headed out there one evening, just before dark, with the re-supply chopper.

Our trip actually started on a sour note as we waited on the helicopter landing pad at the far corner of the base. There were several other GIs lounging in the area, probably waiting for the same chopper to pick them up and ferry them to the field. Suddenly there were shots cracking overhead, apparently coming from a clump of trees 200 yards in front of us. As far as we could tell they were AK-47 rounds, but we couldn't be sure. After a half dozen shots were fired, there was silence. One by one the men on the landing zone, hiding in a variety of places, began to reappear. In a minute or two we were back in our old spots, talking and relaxing as though nothing had happened.

I watched the tree line for the next 30 minutes, hoping to spot some movement, but there was none. It was like other times in the field when I heard shots, but didn't know where they were coming from or for whom they were meant. The same thing had happened to every man who had ever gotten close to the field. Sometimes it was a genuine sniper incident, but most often it was just a platoon of GIs clearing an area by shooting it up. Occasionally it was a band of ARVN troops, blasting away at birds or tin cans. Rifles, to a lot of our Vietnamese comrades, were irresistible toys.

The Huey finally arrived to pick us up, along with a couple of other GIs and several containers of hot food. In about ten minutes we were at the firebase, shaking hands with a lieutenant who showed us to a tent near the LZ headquarters.

We shared a hot meal with the men, and then headed off to our tent around 7:00 P.M. It was already dark, and we were both too tired to catch anyone for an interview. We figured that could wait until morning.

The tent was able to accommodate at least four men, but it was empty except for our two cots, and it had a dirt floor. It was so close to the edge of a steep slope that we were almost too afraid to go out after dark for fear of falling off the fire-base. I smoked a cigarette while Fedo unpacked his poncho and blanket and made up his bed. I peeked outside and noticed that a swarm of clouds had surrounded the base camp, creating a soft screen between us and the valley below. It gave me an eerie feeling of isolation.

I was sure that if an attack came there would be no chance to call for help. With the firebase virtually hidden behind a wall of low-lying clouds, no choppers were going to come out before morning. I was glad that the firebase was so high up, and located on such a steep hill. If the NVA wanted us, they'd have to go straight up. I hoped that would be enough to discourage them.

We were so close to the base radio that we could hear every incoming trans-mission. That allowed us to listen in on a horror story that unfolded shortly after 8:00 P.M. A GI in one of the field companies had gone out from the perimeter to relieve himself. When he returned someone challenged him, and when he didn't answer, he was shot and killed. The man who fired the shot scramble forward and found out that he had killed an American.

The radio made it clear that the platoon was in for a rough night. The GI who had shot his buddy wanted to kill himself. It took several men to keep him from doing it.

No one knew why the man outside the perimeter didn't answer the challenge, but his mistake had cost him his life. Still, he could have been a VC with grenades or a satchel charge. The man who called out to him had no choice but to shoot, but it was hard to convince him of that. There in the darkness, and with no words capable of consoling the survivor, the nightmare seemed to be magnified. The GI was on the verge of going berserk, and we listened helplessly as the company commander and the firebase exchanged information. The company wanted some guidance, but the firebase had none. Just keep him away from anyone's M-16, they said.

It was hours before the man regained his composure. By morning he seemed to have recovered from the shock of the previous night.

After breakfast, I found the lieutenant in charge of the computer. His name was Fitzgerald. He called the computer "Freddie." He told me all about how the "modern" Army was learning to utilize the computer to make its artillery more accurate. I took my notes and wrote a short story when we returned. Fedo took some pictures and even drummed up a cartoon. It showed a computer with a long gun barrel sticking out its front. Later, the story and cartoon ran in our brigade paper.

About a month later we returned to the same firebase. In the meantime, it had been attacked and nearly overrun by a squad of NVA sappers, according to reports.

"A bunch of 'em died right down there," a GI told us after we landed. "They were right by the helicopter pad when they got blown away."

The attack had been ill-planned and totally unsuccessful, but it demonstrated one thing to Fedo and me: the steep slopes hadn't been enough to discourage the NVA. We spent one nervous night lying on rubber mattresses outside a perimeter bunker, and the next day we caught the first chopper home.

ℭ

It was sometime near the end of March when I got a chance to break my first big story. One morning I read in the reports that C Company, 3/1, had tangled with an NVA company and came away with 32 kills. It was by far the biggest single kill for one company in months.

By that time I had replaced Nord on the nightly reports, and I was working from noon until eight each evening. Lieutenant Cobb wanted someone else to do the story, since I wasn't usually around in the morning, but I told him I'd do it on my own time. That impressed him. He liked men who volunteered.

I immediately called the company and found out that a re-supply chopper was leaving at 7:00 A.M. the next day for the field. A colonel would be on the chopper, too, and I was welcome to spend an hour with the company before the chopper returned to Duc Pho.

I had someone wake me the next morning, and 15 minutes later I was waiting in full gear on the chopper pad. We headed north up the coast, maybe two or three miles. We sat down near a line of pine trees just 100 feet from the ocean. The men were waiting there for their hot breakfast.

The company commander, a lieutenant who had taken command when the captain was wounded during the previous day's action, welcomed me. He seemed to be flattered by the fact that a reporter had come to the field to see him and his men, and he did everything he could to cooperate. I told him that I just wanted to wander around, talking with several men about the fight they had been in a few days earlier.

The lieutenant first introduced me to a sergeant sitting nearby, and several other men gathered around with their paper plates as we began to talk. They said the company had walked into an enemy base camp, and fortunately, the company only lost one man in the encounter. He had been hit in the neck with an AK-47 round when he stood up to get a better look. The company, while suffering that lone fatality, counted 32 NVA bodies that evening when the firing had stopped. They admitted that gunships, probably sharks and cobras from Duc Pho, had been responsible for most of the enemy kills. But it was clear that they were proud of the encounter, and quite anxious to talk about it.

I pulled together most of the story before the chopper finished warming up. It wasn't long before we were back in Duc Pho.

I took a full day to write the story, and although it didn't rival Tony's feat, it made the brigade newspaper, the *Army Times*, and the *MACV Reporter*. I was more than satisfied.

One other story that held a lot of promise began to take shape just south of Chu Lai in a place called the Batangan Peninsula. Companies from the 11th Brigade were involved in a sweep of the area, which was designed to purge several villages of Vietcong influence. One of the villages was Pinkville, the place where D Company had run into so much bad luck a few months earlier. Ironically, D Company was involved again as one of the outfits spearheading the drive east toward the ocean.

Somehow the word about the big sweep leaked out, and by the time the brigade was ready to move, Batangan was alive with booby traps and snipers. The villagers had long since fled in boats.

Fedo and I volunteered to go north to cover the brigade's activities. I was hungry for another story, and Fedo was just looking for a way to get out of the office for a few days. We flew to Chu Lai in a mail chopper and went immediately to the division PIO office. There we met a new GI named Dennis, who was assigned the job of finding quarters for us that night.

Since it was Sunday the PIO and some other men in the headquarters company were having a cookout, just 200 yards from the ocean. It was a beautiful evening, with the sun slowly setting on an ocean that glistened with a multitude of colors in the background. The air was filled with the smell of steaks cooking over an open fire. Several of the men were playing a game of volleyball, something we had never seen in Duc Pho. The whole thing made me envious, but Fedo assured me that Chu Lai was a lot more "chicken" that Duc Pho.

"Too much spit shinin'," he said. "They even have inspections once a month. You wouldn't want to live here."

Dennis filled us with steak and Coke that night and took us to his hootch a half-mile from the PIO office. It was basically the same as our hootch back in Duc Pho, but somehow it seemed nicer and certainly cleaner. Each man has his own area, separating him from the next man by plywood walls, almost all covered with Playboy pinups and pictures from back home. There was also a television, something I had never seen anywhere in Duc Pho. I spent much of the night watching movies while Fedo visited some friends up the road. I kept thinking how far away the field was, and how lucky I had been to be away from the PIO.

We ate breakfast in a giant mess hall the next morning, much bigger and much nicer than the one back in Duc Pho. An hour later we caught a ride in a chopper heading toward Batangan. We joined some GIs on the ground who were moving east. It was, by coincidence, my old company, the same one that I had left behind a few months earlier. Virtually all of the old faces were gone. These were younger men, wide-eyed boys in uniforms that looked like they were in the field for the first time. They were brand new, and I pitied them all as I watched them walk by me. At 21, I felt several years older.

I stopped one of the sergeants and asked where a man named Wells might be patrolling. He told me that Wells, and four other GIs, had been killed when one of them tripped a booby trap a day or two earlier.

I thought back to a long conversation Wells and I had up on Cork one afternoon. He was from Illinois, and he was married. What struck me was that he didn't seem to have any fear for the war. He impressed me as one man who would make it home, no matter how much action the company saw during his tour.

When the company finally stopped for the night Fedo and I sat down near an old, abandoned stone house. We ate some C-rations and thought about taking some pictures, but we were too afraid of the booby traps to walk around, so we just shot pictures of one another.

Although we had requested a ride back to Chu Lai that night, we were told that there would be no chopper arriving until morning. We resigned ourselves to spending the night with D Company, even though we were very anxious to get back to a safer area, particularly after hearing about Wells.

As we were sitting and waiting, taking turns paging through the Christmas issue of *Playboy Magazine*, we heard a shot from the opposite side of the house. In a minute the radio nearby was alive with conversation. One of the men on the perimeter, who had been cleaning his M-16 as he stood in a shallow foxhole, suddenly caught a glimpse of movement to his right. He whirled instinctively and fired a single round, striking a Vietcong sapper in the head. The man fell 25 feet away, clutching a grenade in his hand. He died a few minutes later.

By sheer luck, a re-supply chopper showed up just before dark, and we scrambled aboard for a ride north to the comforts of Chu Lai. As I looked down I could see that the company was no more than 100 yards from the ocean. Operation Batangan Peninsula was rapidly coming to a close.

We spent a full day in Chu Lai, waiting for a ride back to Duc Pho. We wandered over to the PX for about an hour, and stood looking at the variety of goods offered for sale there, from Vietnamese trinkets to large stereo systems. There was even a civilian at a desk just outside the door, taking orders from GIs for Ford Pintos. For less that $2,000 a man could have a new card waiting for him when he got back home. At the time I thought it was a great service, a favor that Ford was doing for its men in uniform. But I wasn't ready to commit that kind of money for anything, not until I was sure I had made it through my tour.

Later that day we walked along the road near the beach and found the first USO I had seen since my days at Ft. Polk. There were only a handful of GIs inside, along with a couple of young American women dressed in blue uniforms. Next to the door was a poster advertising flowers that could be ordered in Vietnam and delivered back home. I ordered roses for my mother, and another type of flower for my two grandmothers. They wrote a month later and said the flowers had arrived. I figured it was the best money I had ever spent, in or out of Vietnam.

We finally made our way home by catching rides along Highway 1. The trip had been a failure, for all particle purposes. We didn't come up with a single story or picture. For some reason, Cobb didn't seem to mind. He told us to do better the next time we went out. We assured him that we would.

Chapter 8

Rockets, Like Rain

Until the night of February 23, 1969, Duc Pho was a glorious haven from the war. It provided me with the kind of protection that had only been a dream while I was in the field. I was still vulnerable, of course, but much of the violence and suffering was now buffered by the infantry companies and the firebases that surrounded the brigade headquarters. I felt secure behind my wall of bunkers and claymores and concertina wire. It was as though I had moved from the playing field to the upper deck, like I had become an observer rather than a participant. I had been all but removed from the combat zone, and I liked it that way.

But on February 23, everything changed. I was sitting in the writer's hootch about an hour after supper, sipping a Budweiser with a few other men, when a loud explosion brought us to our feet. I rushed over to the doorway, just in time to see a burst of flames no more than 100 yards away. A second or two later we were in the bunker, trying to figure out what had happened.

We sat quietly for about ten minutes, waiting for something else to happen. By then it was nearly dark, and Duc Pho seemed to be unusually quiet. We decided that the explosion was an enemy round, maybe an RPG, but we were puzzled by the fact that it seemed to be over so quickly. There were no noises, and absolutely no movement anywhere.

As we waited in the bunker, Tony suddenly decided that he needed a piece of the spent RPG round as a souvenir. He wrapped a poncho around his bare chest, jumped into his boots, and raced out the door in his green boxer shorts. In a minute he was checking the area where the rocket landed with a flashlight, trying to find a chunk of metal. A short time later he returned, holding a bit of gray shrapnel in his hand.

What Tony didn't know at the time was that he had nearly lost his life going out into the night for his memorabilia. Two nervous company clerks had been watching from their doorway when they saw a dark figure wearing a flowing cape racing by. They raised their M-16s and nearly fired, deciding at the last minute that the strangely dressed individual was a GI.

A half-hour later a few lights went on around the camp, and we returned to the hootch and opened a few more beers. We soon forgot about the attack.

But around 11:00 P.M. more rounds started coming in, and we scrambled back into the bunker. The rounds were hitting all around us with great frequency. It had rained a day earlier, and the mortars struck the earth with a dull thud. They came so close that mud flew into the bunker and struck one of the men as he sat on the ground. He feigned indignation, saying that the mortar attack was bad enough, but that the mud bath only added insult to injury. We all laughed. The sudden attack, after all, hadn't left anyone injured or dead. We still felt secure, even to the point of joking about what was going on outside.

At first we thought the VC had lobbed in a few rounds just to remind us that they were out there. But after several minutes, we changed our mind. The rounds, both mortars and rockets, kept coming. The thuds were joined by white, flashing explosions that sent loud, echoing noises throughout the base camp. It was as though a squadron of bombers was circling overhead, dropping its payload in a steady stream.

The carefree conversation in the bunker stopped. I closed my eyes and tried to pretend I was somewhere else.

The next day it was estimated that around 200 rockets and mortars had fallen on Duc Pho that night. The attack had lasted no more than an hour, but it seemed much longer. Although the headquarters area had escaped with minor damage, mostly small shrapnel holes in the sides of the hootches, other areas hadn't been so lucky. My old company area, for example, had been hit hard. Someone said a surgeon had lost most of his right hand when a mortar crashed through his hootch. There had also been some fatalities. I stayed out of that area for weeks. I had no interest in seeing the destruction firsthand.

February 23 had signaled the beginning of the Post-Tet. Apparently it was a show of strength by the VC and NVA, but unlike the one in 1968, this offensive used hardware instead of manpower to make its point.

I was sure that Lyndon Johnson's decision to stop the bombing nine months earlier had been the reason for the heavy rocket and mortar attacks. When the bombing had been called off, I was one of those who cheered as I went through my training at Ft. Polk. Now, I wasn't so sure it was a good idea.

The rockets came back on February 27, and again on February 29. Nine more attacks were recorded in Duc Pho during March, including three on the 20th. The security of Duc Pho had all but disappeared. Now, even the grunts didn't want to spend much time there.

The mortars were bad enough, but the rockets generated a special kind of fear. They whistled as they flew in, sending men scrambling in all directions to avoid the deadly shrapnel. We were told that 140mm rockets stood six feet high and carried 25 pounds of explosives. No duds fell in our area, so we never got to see one close up, and that added to the mystery. We felt like sitting ducks. Duc Pho was a stationary target that couldn't be camouflaged. And the worst part was the fact that we were nearly defenseless against the rockets. They came from bamboo barrels up to seven miles away, and they could be moved quite easily.

By the time the choppers left Duc Pho the culprits were already hiding in the jungle. The only defense was a solid bunker, but the PIO hootches, unfortunately, flanked one of the oldest bunkers in the entire camp. It had two layers of sandbags on its roof, and we knew that it would take at least six layers to stop a direct hit by one of those rockets. But we were afraid to pile any more weight onto it, fearing that it would collapse on our heads. We just prayed that the rockets would never hit there.

The rockets always came without warning. Sometimes they fell as we ate lunch. Sometimes we were working at our typewriters. Other attacks interrupted our movies, or scared us out of the latrine. But the most frightening attacks came at night as we slept in our hootches. We'd wake up to the loud explosions, and look through the dust-covered screen doors to white flashes just up the road. When that happened we'd run for the bunker, tripping over one another in near panic. There we'd stand in our shorts and bare feet, hoping that the attack would soon end, and cursing the NVA for scaring us half to death and robbing us of our sleep. A few minutes later someone would get tired of waiting and go back to bed, and it wasn't long before the rest of us followed.

I remember several attacks very distinctly. In addition to the rounds that came in after dark, we also experienced several during the day. One day, around noon, I was walking up to the PIO hootch after finishing lunch when a couple of 140mm rockets whistled in. There was a two or three-foot ditch running parallel with the road, and it would have made an instant and convenient shelter, but I broke into a run and didn't stop until I had joined the other men in the little darkroom next to the hootch. I knew, even at the time, that it didn't make any sense. I should have dropped into the ditch and stayed there. But it was that fear of being alone that drove me to seek out the other men. I simply didn't have the courage to wait out an attack by myself.

Another time they came in just as we were cleaning our trays behind the mess hall. There were three of them, and we heard each one as it sailed overhead. We all ducked to the ground, and leftover food went in all directions. It looked like a cut from some old Three Stooges movie.

The attacks came only about once every five days during April and May, but the fear of them dominated our lives. We were a fairly small target, and we thought it was only a matter of time before one of the rounds hit either the writers' or the photographers' hootches. We figured the NVA were usually aiming for the brigade headquarters, a reinforced bunker just about 300 yards from our office. One night they even managed to drop a round on it. It blew away some sandbags, and cracked a beam or two, but otherwise did no damage. The ceiling held, and the men inside were unhurt.

I made only one phone call home during those tense weeks. I requested a line through to the states around noon one day, but it didn't come in until 2:00 A.M. the next morning. I talked with my mother and father for several minutes, trying desperately to overcome the beer that was still swimming around in my brain. I told them everything was going fine, and that I was looking forward to coming home. At least, I thought they knew that I was alive and relatively well.

The days went by quickly, but the evenings, from dark until we turned in, were agonizingly long. I usually drank around a six-pack of beer and chewed on some corn curls or ate a can of beans to pass the time. Tony had a tape recorder he brought back form R and R in March, and it served as a pleasant diversion. He had the Everly Brothers and the Association, and we played them over and over every night for hours. Occasionally the reels would come undone, and Tony, full of beer and with a cigarette constantly dangling from his mouth, would labor until the reel was either fixed or he became too frustrated to continue.

At other times we'd strum on guitars and sing a few songs. But there was always that single thought in the back of our minds that a rocket could sail in at any moment. We were like children again, with our fear multiplying after the sun went down. As we sat in our hootch beneath that single light bulb, we often fell silent at the slightest noise. There were several false starts. We often broke for the bunker, and then realized a minute or two later that nothing was happening. We'd laugh and go back to our beer and music, relieved but no less alert for the next sound outside the hootch.

By the end of May our hootch was peppered with shrapnel holes from incoming rounds. Lockers were also penetrated, with one chunk of shrapnel narrowly missing Tony's tape deck.

But we were lucky. Occasionally a round caused fatalities in another part of the firebase. We heard about the deaths and injuries through the grapevine. During one attack, for example, a rocket crashed through a tent and landed on a table where five GIs were playing poker. Four of them died.

One other time the chaplain's hootch, which was directly behind the PIO office, took an RPG round. It sailed through the screen door, making a hole no larger than a silver dollar. But its power amazed us. The round stuck the chaplain's desk, a sturdy metal structure, and ripped it into two pieces. It was as though a giant had picked it up and simply torn it apart. The phone was nowhere in sight. We finally located it overhead, dangling from the ceiling.

The rockets also did their share of psychological damage. After a few weeks the tension began to wear on all of us. One night, after a long session of beer drinking, we turned out the lights about eleven. But two men, Tony from Texas and Sergeant Deverick from Illinois, began to argue. Tony said the best looking women in America lived in Texas; Deverick said they were in Illinois. The argument went on for several minutes, with each man literally screaming in an effort to win the ludicrous debate. Finally, Deverick jumped out of his bunk, picked up a mess kit knife, and started toward Tony's bed. He stopped halfway, tossing the knife on the table.

"What am I doing?" he said.

He crawled back into bed, and the argument ended.

The tension got to other men in the camp, too. One night, according to the stories we heard, a GI on the perimeter left his bunker to relieve himself. As he walked back into the dark bunker the other man on guard shot and killed him. Then, in a state of panic, he raced to the next bunker, only to be killed by a third GI who had heard the first shot.

The perimeter was the closest I got to the action while I was with the PIO, except for my short jaunts in the field. The guard roster was pretty constant. I had to spend a night in a bunker every other week. The other men in the PIO had the same responsibility.

It was usually a pretty quiet night. But one evening, around seven-thirty, something happened that threw a new scare into all of us. Jim Rose, our office typist, was one of three men in a bunker on the south end of the perimeter when it was hit by an RPG round. The flash in the distance was all they saw. In a second the wall of the bunker was exploding. Fortunately, the round buried itself in the sandbags. There was nothing but a flash and a loud boom. But it was more than enough for the three men on guard. They said their ears hurt, and they were allowed to go back to their hootches.

I wandered back to the writer's hootch and found Lieutenant Peleate standing in the doorway, wearing his helmet and flak jacket. He said he needed three men to take over the bunker for the rest of the night. He seemed unusually serious, almost scared.

Tony, already on his way to a big drunk, volunteered. So did Fedo. For some reason I decided to go along. I guess I was taken with a sense of adventure. Maybe some of my old hero complex was returning. I guess I had been out of the field too long.

We settled in the bunker and divided up our time into equal parts. When my guard was over I lay down on the wall that had been hit, finding it a very comfortable place to sleep. Fedo stayed awake all night. He said he had been too concerned about another attack to close his eyes.

Later, in the same bunker, I had a much more frightening experience. One night, late in April, while I was pulling one of my regular guard stints, Duc Pho was attacked by rockets and PRG rounds. Earlier that day rumors had been circulating that an attack was imminent. Intelligence was right on the button with its prediction. It was around 11:00 P.M. when we began to take rounds. We could hear explosions behind us, and a few seconds later we saw the flashes in the distance. There were two other men in the bunker with me, both younger and much newer in the country. I immediately lowered my M-16 and fired off a clip, and they did the same. I quickly loaded a second clip of 20 rounds, and ran it off on automatic, trying to zero in on the flashes. On our right, and left, .50 caliber machine guns were spitting tracer rounds in the same direction. As we shot we could hear the PRG rounds sailing over our heads and landing hundreds of yards inside the perimeter.

After about ten rounds, the attack ended. It had lasted only about a minute, probably less.

The rest of the night was quiet, and we returned to our normal guard schedule. But, for that single minute, I felt as though I was standing toe to toe with the NVA, trying desperately to kill something in the black of the night before it killed me. I had little hope of finding the target. There was no way to judge distance, and in my hurry to put out rounds, I didn't bother to take a deliberate aim. I just fired away, wanting the whole thing to end before an RPG found my bunker and blew me to bits.

I wasn't hesitant, in the least, about killing someone that night. If I would have had to kill 50 NVA to save myself, I wouldn't have given it a second thought. With every passing moment the goal of getting home alive became more and more of an obsesssion. I had invested too much in my tour to let it all go down the drain in a single, short-lived attack.

ॐ

The rocket attacks frustrated everyone. They made us feel helpless, totally helpless. But every once in a while the gunships would give some hint that we might be turning things around.

One day, after a fierce attack on Duc Pho, including several rockets, RPGs, and mortar rounds, my evening check of the activity board showed 30 NVA kills a few miles north of Duc Pho. The kills were in the same area where the rockets had come from the previous night. The report also said that several bamboo poles were spotted, probably the ones used to aim the rockets.

I saw it as one of the better stories to come along in several weeks, and I talked Cobb into letting me have it. I began to search for the pilot of the gunship who had been responsible for most of the enemy KIAs.

I found him just up the road, maybe a quarter of a mile east of the PIO hootch. He was around 26, mature-looking and professional. He was calm and businesslike, clearly no wide-eyed draftee who had been drawn into the war by sheer bad luck. He was obviously a career man on the way up.

At first he was hesitant about talking, but he was soon describing how the enemy troops had been spotted, and how he opened up on them with rockets and machine gun fire, killing them quickly.

I took notes furiously, certain that my story was destined for a prominent spot in the next issue of *Stars and Stripes*.

When we finished I put away my pen and folded up my notebook. I thanked him for his time and his story. But as I turned to walk away he said something that turned everything upside down.

"Don't put this in," he said, smiling with a touch of embarrassment, "but most of them were women and kids."

I was stunned, but I nodded meekly and walked off. I could hardly believe what he said. As I walked up the road toward the PIO hootch, I tried to sort it out. Everyone knew that a lot of the Vietcong were women, but what about the kids? Had we descended to making war on children, even if they were a party to the rocket attacks?

I never wrote a single sentence about the interview. The thought of children being gunned down by an American helicopter sickened me. I wished I had never even met the pilot. I put the whole affair out of my mind.

It was actually years before I figured out what had really happened that night in the field. The Vietnamese were incredible scavengers, always tagging along with American units to pick up their trash. The women and children that were found at the rocket site were doing the same thing. The choppers didn't get there until several hours after the attack. The Vietnamese were nothing more than unlucky civilians, caught in the wrong place at the wrong time. Being there when the choppers arrived had cost them their lives.

The whole thing was pure insanity. But after ten or eleven months in Vietnam, insanity seemed to be more and more normal. One night, for example, Lieutenant Cobb was struck in the face by a stray bullet. He was sitting at his desk when the bullet came through the back of the hootch and creased his chin. It whirled him around and he landed at the feet of another man standing nearby.

Cobb, only slightly injured, put a handkerchief over his chin and headed for the door. I met him just as he came down the steps.

"What happened?" I asked.

"I just got shot."

"Where are you going?"

"To get my purple heart."

Cobb was the second man to stop a bullet while he was in the PIO hootch. Two months earlier, Nord was standing next to me when he felt a sting on his back. We heard something drop into the typewriter a second later. He took off his shirt and found a little red spot just below his neck. Tony hunted for 30 minutes before he pulled an M-16 slug from inside the typewriter. The round had been shot into the air, and its fall was broken only by the canvas tent above us.

Lieutenant Peleate also had a close call. He was away from his desk one morning when a bullet came flying through the office and tore a hole in the wooden frame directly behind his chair. If he had been sitting there, he would have been killed.

It was all insanity, of course. Bullets, some shot intentionally and some shot unintentionally, were coming from all directions. Duc Pho, like most of the rest of Vietnam, was a place where a man had almost as much chance of dying accidentally as he did on purpose. I stopped trying to rationalize the whole affair, trusting instead that I simply wasn't meant to die at the age of 21.

But the insanity of Vietnam, like a contagious disease, had touched us all. Our own bit of craziness, typified by Cobb's rush to pin on his purple heart, prevented us from seeing that the war was insane, too. The fear of dying, alone and in a moment of horrible violence, had warped us all, and the rockets and stray bullets were at least partially to blame. We defended ourselves with jokes about death. We had come to accept a world at war as a normal world. It would take years before we would realize that we had been temporarily mad.

CR

I suggested to the other men in the PIO one day that the bunker might be made safer if we just piled sandbags on it west end. I had been watching the activity board for several weeks, and noted that most of the attacks came from the west. If a missile sailed in from that direction, it would probably destroy the west wall with a direct hit. Reinforcing that side of our vital shelter would add to our safety, even if we couldn't pile more sandbags on the roof where extra layers were badly needed.

The other men agreed, and we began one night, filling and stacking sandbags by the light of a single bulb. A few of us worked an hour or two for about ten days straight. We finally got bored and gave up, but not before we had filled around a hundred bags and packed them loosely against the wall. It wasn't much, we thought, but it mitigated our feelings of helplessness. At least we had done something to try to buffer the feared rocket attacks.

The rockets often came in little bunches, maybe three at a time, and seldom more than once a day. But once, late in May, we were attacked during the day and again that night, and it was the latter incident that nearly brought our morale to the breaking point. Men raced from the two hootches around 10:00 P.M. when the first whistle and explosion rocked the camp. It was followed by more rockets and RPG rounds, and a few mortars. It went on for several minutes, then stopped, and then continued. Some of the rounds landed fairly close, booming with an ear-shattering intensity.

There were around twelve of us, huddled in a 15 by 15 bunker with our M-16s, wondering if a round was headed our way that would chew out a piece of the sand-bagged walls and leave us peppered with chunks of hot shrapnel. The night was pitch black, and silent. The rounds were coming in, but there was no answer from the camp. No machinegun fire. No artillery barrages. Nothing. It was as though the whole firebase was hiding and waiting for the NVA to run out of rockets and RPGs. We were like a fighter, backed into a corner with his arms covering his face, waiting for his opponent to punch himself out. For the first time I felt as though our overwhelming fire power had been badly exaggerated.

After the second or third barrage that evening someone opened a Bible and began to read it by flashlight. It helped for a few minutes, but I soon lost my concentration. I couldn't think about anything but the fury of the attack.

The incoming rounds finally stopped, and a half hour later we were back in the hootches, drinking beer and listening to music. We found solace in pretending that nothing had happened.

ᏋᎵ

The bunker was one place in camp where I felt even remotely safe. It was built at ground level, and it was badly in need of reinforcement, but it was surely better than sleeping in a hootch with nothing but a canvas roof overhead.

So I thought it only made good sense to spend as much time in the bunker as possible. Around the end of April, with five weeks left on my tour, I moved my bed out of the hootch and into the bunker. It was actually cooler that in the hootch. Except for the possible invasion of snakes or rodents during the night, it was easily as comfortable. A couple of weeks later Jim Rose, the typist, joined me there. He brought a fan and an electric cord with him, and that made the hot spring nights much more tolerable. The fan rotated from side to side, spraying my bunk with a cool breeze every five or ten seconds.

After that, when the rockets would rain in on Duc Pho, we played host to the other men as they scrambled into the bunker. Some would go back to bed almost immediately after an attack, but others would remain for hours, talking with Rose and me.

Chapter 9
Three Days to Freedom

On the morning of June 3, 1968, I had just three days left on my tour in Vietnam. It was hot, as usual, and the sky was perfectly clear and blue. All I could think about was the fact that I would only have to spend one more night in Duc Pho. The next one would be spent in Chu Lai, probably in the PIO hootch in front of a television set, surrounded by *Playboy* magazines and cold beers.

I spent the day in the PIO hootch, watching the other men as they worked. I tried to busy myself with a story, but it was no use; I was too preoccupied with the thought of leaving.

The day actually went by rather quickly. I made a trip down to my old company in an effort to retrieve my medical records, but the clerk told me that they had been lost. He said if I could wait around for a few more days they might be able to come up with them. I told them to forget it. I was one day away from leaving the 11th Brigade behind for good.

I spent the early evening in the bunker, watching the sun go down. I had been unable to eat for two days. My stomach was in a knot. I tried an occasional Coke, and later threw them up. I smoked now and then, but it gave me no satisfaction. I found myself thinking of nothing but the rocket attacks and surviving for another twelve hours. My anxiety was growing by leaps and bounds. I could hardly stand to be inside my own skin.

About 30 minutes before dark, Fedo and some of the other men started an impromptu baseball game outside the bunker. They tried to get me to join them, and although I hesitated, in a few minutes I was standing near home plate, waiting for my turn at bat. I thought it would help to pass the time.

I stroked a single and a double, and by the third time I stepped to the plate I had almost forgotten where I was.

But then it happened. I heard two thumps behind some hootches. I dropped my bat and ran for the nearest bunker. No one else moved. They just laughed and called me "short timer." But a second or two later there were two muffled booms in the distance, the kind of noises that rockets made when they were launched several miles away.

All of the other men suddenly rushed for the bunker and dove inside. It was a beautifully reinforced, underground bunker constructed for the Korean tailors, with four wooden steps leading from ground level to its dirt floor. Fedo was the last man to make it to the door, and he dove head first as the whistles became louder and louder, finally turning into explosions. I lifted my head to an opening in time to see a puff of black smoke slowly curling upward, just a few feet from where I had been standing at home plate.

I slumped to the ground, my chest covered with sweat. I was instantly exhausted and limp, like a man who had just completed a marathon run. The other men stood in the center of the little bunker, listening carefully for more rounds. I felt sorry for them, because I was sure Duc Pho hadn't yet seem its worst days. I was due to go home to Chu Lai in twelve hours, but they had to stay behind. I wished them luck. I was sure they would need it.

One by one we raced back to the PIO bunker. I was the last man to leave. I sat alone for five minutes, pondering the possibility of staying in the Korean bunker overnight. After all, I told myself, it could take a rocket and survive, while the PIO hootch could not. Common sense told me to stay put, but I couldn't help myself. I needed the reassurance of the other men too much to isolate myself.

There may have been a second rocket attack that night, but I was never sure. It seemed like I heard rounds falling several hours after we turned in, but it may have been a dream. I didn't even bother to ask anyone the next day. I guess I was too afraid to find out that the noises I heard in my sleep were real.

One June 4th I sat around the office, calling every half hour to find out when a chopper would be leaving Duc Pho. I was sure there would be several flights to Chu Lai that day, but by 3:00 P.M. I still hadn't found any transportation. I began to get worried, and that worry soon became a gnawing fear. In a couple of hours the commuting choppers would stop, and I would have to spend another night in the PIO bunker. I felt certain that another attack was coming, and equally certain that I might not be able to take even a single rocket exploding near me. I was like a man on a runaway roller coaster. I was sure I was on the verge of cracking up. I had to find a chopper. There was no alternative.

I telephoned again and again. Finally I was told that a re-supply helicopter was going to Chu Lai around 4:00 P.M. I packed my gear and hurriedly shook hands with the men in the office, and headed east to the chopper pad. It was 200 yards away, and I was the lone figure on an open space the size of a football field. If a rocket came in there would be nowhere to hide. I prayed silently that any attack would wait at least until after dark.

The sun was dropping in the west as the chopper revved up and lifted off the pad. In a minute I was high over Duc Pho. For the first time in a year I felt as though I had made it out of Vietnam alive.

That night, the men in the Chu Lai PIO found an empty bunk for me, and I followed Dennis over to the enlisted men's club. I called Duc Pho and talked with Lieutenant Cobb, thanking him over and over again for getting me out of the field. He said no rockets had fallen yet that night. I wished him luck on the rest of his tour.

Chapter 10

Winners and Losers

An aging general was once asked if he minded getting old. He just laughed.

"Oh, no," he said. "It's like climbing a mountain. The higher you get, the farther you see.'

I'm a long way from my one-year tour in Vietnam, but in some ways I can see it more clearly now than I did when came home over three decades ago. Since returning to the U.S., I've gotten married and had children, earned college degrees, and enjoyed four different careers. I've written five books, interviewed famous people like Dr. Ben Spock and Dr. Ruth Westheimer, and been involved in a lawsuit that was appealed all the way to the U.S. Supreme Court. I've visited places from coast to coast, ridden a train through the Rocky Mountains, jogged on a July day in Florida, and walked the battlefields of Gettysburg.

I'm both a winner and loser because I went to Vietnam. I've had good days and bad days since coming home, but I've never regretted spending my time there. I tell my students that it was both the best year and the worst year of my life. The Army and the war exposed me to extreme conditions–hunger, thirst, danger and disease–that wouldn't be a part of my life's experiences if I hadn't gone overseas. It stretched my "life's circle" in ways which were sometimes miserable and frightening, but also in ways which gave me a chance to learn just how strong and resilient and resourceful I could be. I witnessed both the savagery and the nobility that young Americans can exhibit under the most extreme conditions.

I also had some good times in Vietnam, and made some lifelong friends. I learned new skills and acquired a brand new career, thanks to a chance meeting with another soldier on a remote firebase back in 1968.

As a veteran, I have been blessed with both state and federal benefits. I used the G.I. Bill to get myself through college; I was even released from the Army three months early to start classes. If I ever get sick, there will be additional benefits from the Veterans Administration and from my own State Department of Veterans Affairs.

Many of the good things that happened to me because of Vietnam wouldn't have happened if I had stayed home and simply put in my time as a clerk-typist at some benign, stateside Army base. For me, Vietnam was the experience of a lifetime, just like it is for most veterans. I've seldom met a man who was sorry he went, no matter how much it hurt or how much of himself he was forced to leave behind.

Of course, I paid a price for going to Vietnam. My battle with malaria and ringworm infection took their toll on me physically, and like so many others, I was exposed to Agent Orange while I was there, the same poison which is now linked to a host of diseases which have killed some veterans and caused birth defects in their children. Only time will tell if my exposure leads to health problems in the future either for me or my children.

I also lost much of my innocence in Vietnam, and at least part of my sense of security. Trust doesn't come as easily as it once did, and I no longer take it for granted that my plane won't crash or that some other driver won't run into car. Vietnam left me with what I call a "healthy case of paranoia." I don't trust strangers and even casual acquaintances like I once did; I certainly don't trust government (at any level) to keep its word, or to deal with me fairly. I've learned to read the fine print before I sign anything.

While the war made me stronger and gave me some of the wisdom that civilian life simply doesn't offer, I don't advocate it for everyone. I certainly don't ever want my two sons or any other young people to have to see and do what I did in Vietnam. My strongest desire is for peace, and for peaceful solutions to international problems, no matter how difficult and complex they may be.

I was once quite angry at the American leaders who sent us to Vietnam, like Lyndon Johnson, and even angrier at those who refused to bring us home after the war had entered a new phase of hopelessness and human sacrifice, like Richard Nixon, but I've mellowed with time. Vietnam took its toll on them, too, just like it did on so many in my baby boomer generation. There was plenty of violence, frustration, and disappointment to go around during the decade in which Americans were fighting and dying for reasons that no one could fully explain or understand.

Vietnam was the first war that America didn't win. It was also a war in which those who participated often shouldered much of the blame. Many anti-war protesters heaped scorn on Vietnam veterans, calling them "baby burners" and "baby killers," while members of veterans organizations like the American Legion and VFW turned a cold shoulder to a generation that seemed to come up short on the battlefield. It's little wonder that most the men who served in Vietnam won't talk about it, won't join their local Legion post, and won't go to Jane Fonda movies.

My own fear is that the lessons of Vietnam, which are numerous and sometimes complex, will be lost on a generation that is both refreshingly objective and understandably curious about it. I see the frustration in the faces of my students, and hear it in their voices. They know better than to believe the "Rambo" stereotype, and the simplistic idea that Vietnam was both a morale and military disaster. But where can they turn for the truth? Who is going to teach them the lessons they need to learn in order to make the right decision when the next crisis comes along?

Please don't blame the veterans for not talking about the war. Some will talk when they're ready; others will take their feelings and experiences to their graves. That's their privilege; they've earned the right to be left alone.

But as a history teacher, I certainly believe that Vietnam has to be kept alive and re-examined from time to time in order to safeguard us from a repeat of that agonizing experience. I also believe that lots of young people owe their lives to the Vietnam War because it has made us think twice about committing troops whenever terrorism, communism, or tyranny bumped up against American interests or American ideals.

Vietnam was a terrible war, but it had a positive side, too.

At least that's what I see, now that I'm getting closer to the top of the mountain.

Glossary

AK47 - The standard infantry rifle carried by VC and NVA and comparable to the M-16. Produced by Russia.

APC - Armored Personnel Carrier, a track combat vehicle to carry troops.

ARVN - South Vietnamese Army, South Vietnamese soldier.

Battalion - American Army unit usually consisting of 500-600 men.

B-52 - Heavy American bomber.

Chinook - Heavy American helicopter for transporting troops and cargo, with blades in front and back.

Chopper - GI slang for all types of helicopters.

CID - Criminal Investigation Division.

CO - Commanding officer.

Company - American Army unit usually consisting of 100-200 men.

C-rations - Canned combat meals, usually carried by infantrymen.

C-4 - Putty-like explosive, often used by GIs to hear C-rations.

C-130 - Fixed wing cargo transport plane.

Gook - Derogatory term referring to Orientals.

Grunt - GI slang for infantryman.

Hootch - Vietnamese hut, also referred to many structures built by Americans to be used as living quarters.

Humping - Hard walking through Vietnam, usually carrying a rucksack.

Huey - Slang for medium-sized helicopter, an Army UH-1, the workhorse in Vietnam.

KP - Kitchen patrol.

LZ - Landing zone.

NCO - Non-commissioned officer, sergeant.

NVA - North Vietnamese Army, North Vietnamese soldier.

PFC - Private First Class, E-3.

PIO - Public Information Office.

Platoon - American Army unit usually consisting of 45-50 men.

POW - Prisoner of war.

Profile - Slang referring to an individual's medical status; usually refers to medical condition, indicating permanent or temporary limitations on duties that the person can perform.

PX - Post Exchange

RAMFs, REMFs - Rear Area Mother Fuckers; Rear Echelon Mother Fuckers.

R and R - Rest and recreation, or rest and recuperation.

Recon Platoon - Reconnaissance platoon, responsible for exploring and breaking territory for other infantry units.

RPG - Rocket-propelled grenade, Russian made.

Specialist 4 - Rank equivalent to corporal.

Squad - The smallest military organization, usually consisting of less than a dozen men.

VC - Vietcong.

Water Buffalo - The work animals of Vietnam; also a two-wheeled trailer carrying 400 gallons of fresh water.

1-A - Eligible for service.

2-S - Student deferment.

4-F - Ineligible for service.

Welcome to Hellgate Press

For Other Perspectives on the Vietnam War,

Consider These Exciting Titles from **Hellgate Press**

The Elephant and the Tiger

The Full Story of the Vietnam War
by Wilbur H. Morrison   ISBN: 1-55571-612-1
730 pages, Paperback: $26.95

The Elephant and the Tiger is a thorough and thought-provoking history of the Vietnam War. It chronicles the events from Dec. 13, 1954, the date when the U.S. first signed a formal agreement with France to assume more responsibility for equipping and training the South Vietnamese armed forces, until 1975 when South Vietnam's army was swept aside by the North Vietnamese and the last Americans were forced to flee the country in defeat. Includes 14 pages of photographs.

Honor & Sacrifice

The Montagnards of Ba Cat, Vietnam
by Anthony J. Blondell   ISBN: 1-55571-533-8
250 pages, Hardcover: $21.95

Special Forces (Green Beret) A-Team member, Anthony Blondell, tells an action-packed story of the exploitation of the Montagnards, and what happens when the South Vietnamese government not only backs out of a nearly completed, $5,000-per-day Special Forces mission, but tries to sabotage it to keep from paying.

Printed in the United States
4145

9 781555 716158